Supporting and Troubleshooting Windows Vista Client

Lab Manual

Supporting and Troubleshooting Windows Vista Client

Lab Manual

OWEN FOWLER

KURT MEYER

WILEY

EXECUTIVE EDITOR	John Kane
SENIOR EDITOR	Gary Schwartz
DIRECTOR OF MARKETING AND SALES	Mitchell Beaton
PRODUCTION MANAGER	Micheline Frederick
PRODUCTION EDITOR	Kerry Weinstein
DEVELOPMENT AND PRODUCTION	Custom Editorial Productions, Inc.

To order books or for customer service, please call 1-800-CALL WILEY (225-5945).

ISBN   978-0-470-11164-2

Printed in the United States of America

10 9 8 7 6 5 4 3 2 1

BRIEF CONTENTS

CONTENTS

LAB 1
PREPARING TO DEPLOY WINDOWS VISTA

This lab contains the following exercises and activities:

BEFORE YOU BEGIN

Lab 1 assumes that setup has been completed as specified in the Setup document. You will be working with a domain named contoso and with a server and client named WinSrv03 and Sales01 respectively. Depending on your lab environment, your instructor might assign you an index that you should append to the server, client, and domain names. The server should already have an account created for Chris Ashton (chrisa), with normal user privileges, and an account created for Network Administrator (netadmin), with full administrator privileges. You will log on as chrisa and use the netadmin account when you need to supply administrator credentials. Passwords for all accounts are identical: p@ssw0rd (where the "0" is a zero).

SCENARIO

You are a network administrator for Contoso, Ltd., a provider of insurance products. In this lab, you will prepare the domain for a Microsoft Windows Vista deployment by setting up basic accounts, shared folders, and policies.

In the Lab Challenge, you will practice saving and restoring user migration data.

After completing this lab, you will be able to:

- Create user accounts and groups.

- Assign group membership.

- Create a network share and set permissions.

- Create a GPO.

- Configure Folder Redirection.

- Save and restore user settings for migration.

Estimated lab time: 50 minutes

Exercise 1.1· Create User Accounts and Groups

Overview	Before a user can log on to a domain, the user account must be created on the domain server. You will create a security group for the sales department (Sales) and a security group for the marketing department (Mktg). You will then create two user accounts, one for salesperson John Tippett (johnt) and one for marketing director Sheela Word (sheelaw). Later you will use these accounts and groups to control each user's environment when they log on to the network from a Windows Vista client. In an enterprise, you will need an account for each individual who logs on to the network, and you will want separate security groups for each set of users with common security or other network administration needs.
Completion time	5 minutes

1. Log on to Windows Server 2003 with your administrator account. (The logon ID is netadmin and password is p@ssw0rd, where the "0" is a zero.)

> **NOTE**
>
> *Although the first three exercises in this lab instruct you to log on to the server, it is always best to administer the server from a Windows Vista client. Typically, you should log on to the client using non-administrator credentials and elevate your credentials only when necessary.*

2. From the Start menu, point to Administrative Tools and then select Active Directory Users And Computers.

3. In the Active Directory Users And Computers console, expand the contoso.com domain if necessary. Then right-click the Users node, point to New, and select Group, as shown in Figure 1-1.

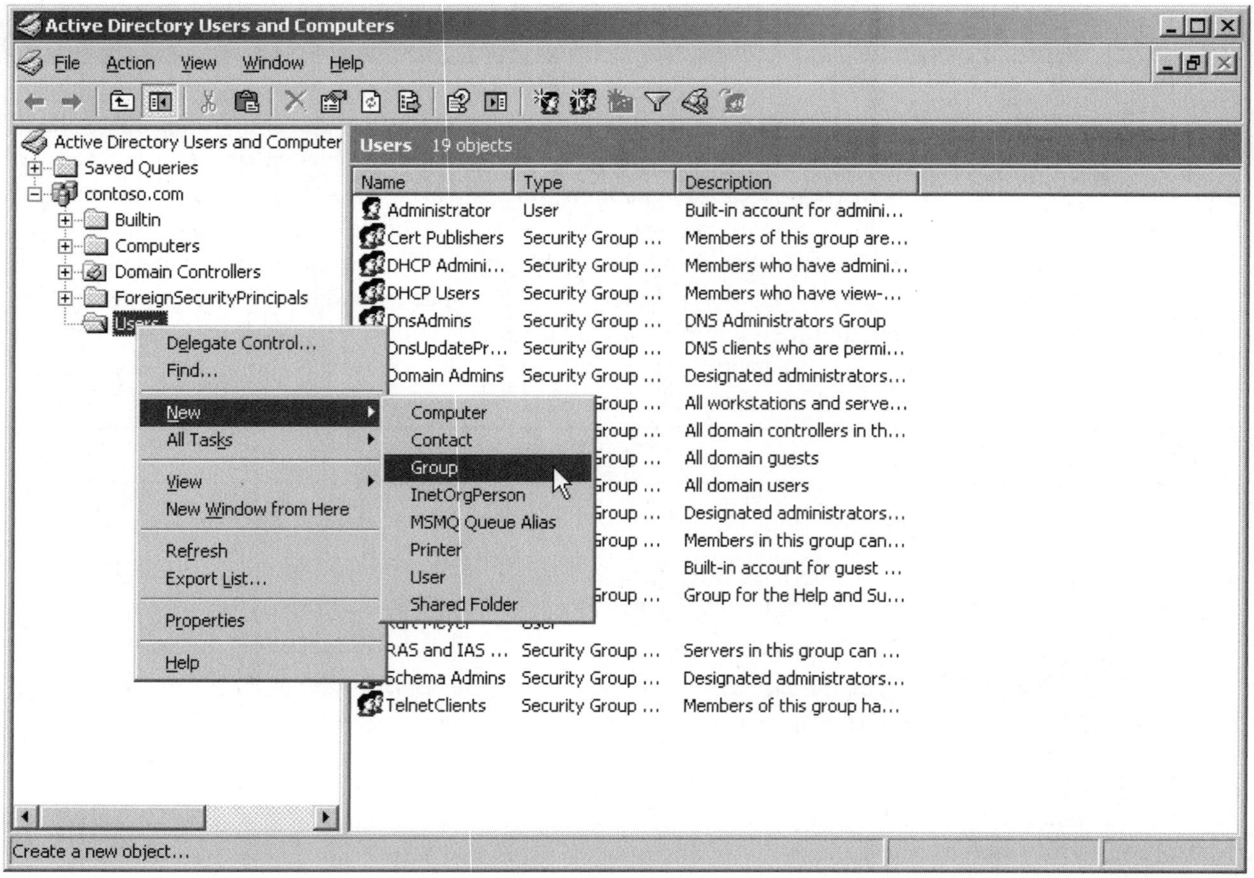

Figure 1-1
The Active Directory Users And Computers console

4. In the New Object – Group dialog box, key **Sales** in the Group Name text box and then click OK.

5. Repeat steps 3 and 4 to add the Mktg group.

6. Right-click the Users node, point to New, and then select User.

7. In the New Object – User dialog box, key **John** in the First Name text box, key **Tippett** in the Last Name text box, and key **johnt** in the User Logon Name text box, as shown in Figure 1-2. Click Next.

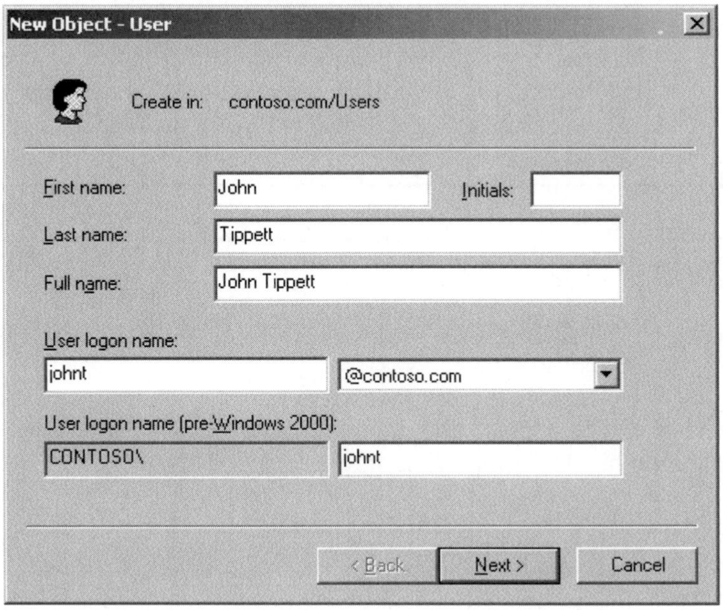

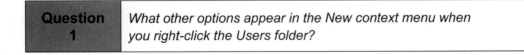

Figure 1-2
The New Object – User dialog box

8. Key and confirm a password in the next New Object – User dialog box. For this manual, use p@ssw0rd (where the "0" is a zero) for all passwords so that they will be easy to remember. Of course, in a real enterprise system you would choose a random password and instruct the user to change it the first time they log on.

9. Select the Password Never Expires checkbox (again as a convenience for working through this manual) and then click OK in the Active Directory message box that pops up.

10. Click Next and then click Finish.

11. Repeat steps 6–10 to create a user account for Sheela Word with the logon name of sheelaw.

Question 1	*What other options appear in the New context menu when you right-click the Users folder?*

Exercise 1.2	Assign Users to Groups
Overview	You will assign the users you created in Exercise 1.1 to two different groups. For this exercise, you will add johnt to the Sales group and sheelaw to the Mktg group. Note that in a typically complex enterprise, individuals are often members of multiple groups. For example, you might create a Managers group, to which sheelaw, being the marketing director, would also be added.
Completion time	2 minutes

1. In the Active Directory Users And Computers console, select the Users node in the tree.

2. Double-click the John Tippett user account in the Details pane. The John Tippet Properties dialog box is displayed, as shown in Figure 1-3.

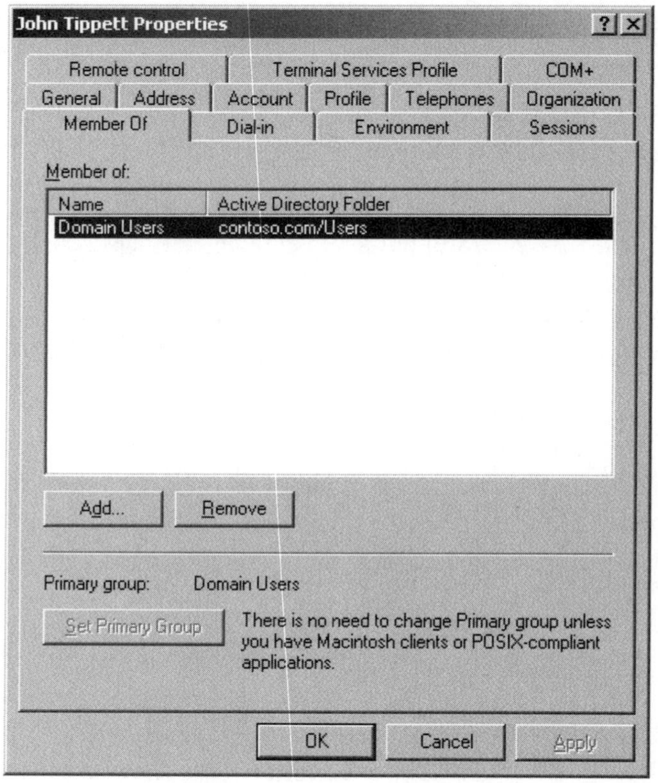

Figure 1-3
The user account Properties dialog box for John Tippet

3. Select the Member Of tab and then click Add. The Select Groups dialog box is displayed.

4. In the Select Groups dialog box, key **Sales** in the Enter The Object Names To Select text box, click Check Names, and then click OK. The Sales group is displayed in the Member Of list box.

5. Click OK to close the John Tippet Properties dialog box.

6. Repeat steps 2–5 to add Sheela Word to the Mktg group.

7. Double-click the Sales group or the Mktg group and then select the Members tab to verify that you have added the appropriate user accounts to each group.

8. Click OK to close the group Properties dialog box.

9. From the File menu, choose Exit to close the Active Directory Users And Computers console.

Question 2	What are some of the built-in security groups already present on the server?

Exercise 1.3   Create Network Shares and Set Permissions

Overview	As preparation for subsequent exercises, you will create network shares and set appropriate permissions. For users to store files on the network server so that the files are accessible to them (sometimes transparently) from all client machines on the network, users must be given appropriate permissions to files on the server, and the files must be correctly shared on the network. You will use the shared folders you set up in this exercise later when you implement Folder Redirection.
Completion time	10 minutes

1. On the server, click Start and then click Windows Explorer.

2. Expand the My Computer node and select the Local Disk (C:) node.

3. Right-click the Details pane, point to New, and then select Folder. Rename the folder **Clients**.

4. Within the Clients folder, create the tree structure, as shown in Figure 1-4.

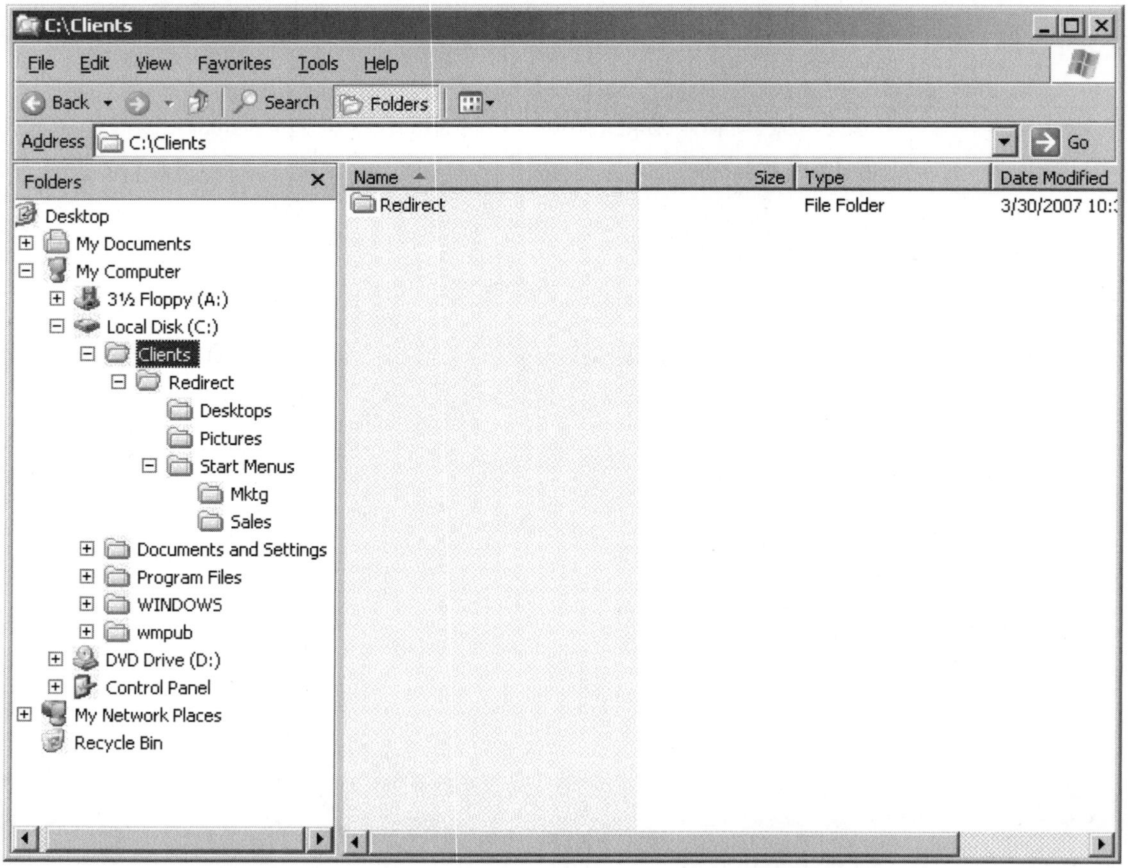

Figure 1-4
Tree structure for Folder Redirection exercises

5. Right-click the Redirect folder and then select Sharing And Security. The Redirect Properties dialog box is displayed.

6. On the Sharing tab of the Redirect Properties dialog box, turn on the Share This Folder option.

7. Click Permissions. The Permissions For Redirect dialog box is displayed, as shown in Figure 1-5.

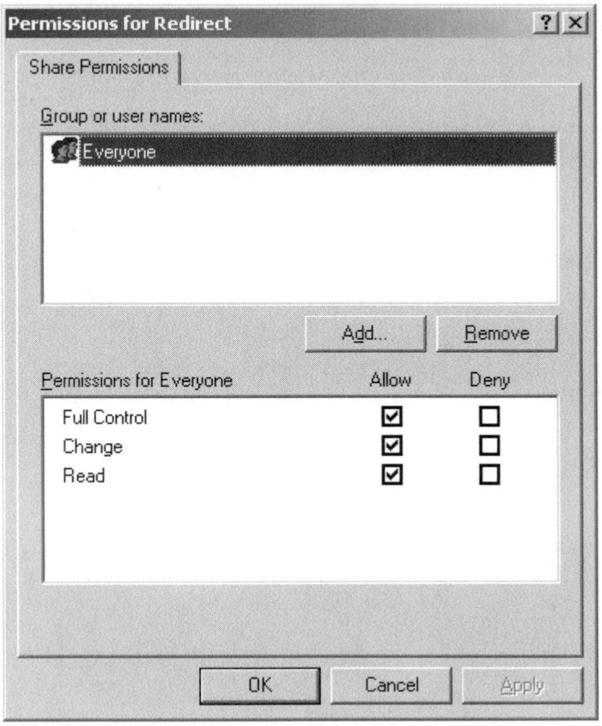

Figure 1-5
The Permissions For Redirect dialog box

8. Select the Allow check box for Full Control and then click OK. This effectively turns off share-level permission checking so that access to the share can be administered solely through security settings.

9. On the Security tab of the Redirect Properties dialog box, click Add. The Select Users, Computers, Or Groups dialog box is displayed.

10. Key **Sales** in the Enter The Object Names To Select text box, click Check Names, and then click OK.

> **NOTE**
>
> *Because sensitive information is often stored in user profiles and in redirected user folders, Microsoft recommends that you restrict access to these folders to the minimum set of users. You might also want to prevent these shares from being visible to users who are browsing network shares. To do so, append a dollar sign ($) to the share name.*
>
> *Do not use Offline Folder Caching or Encrypted File System (EFS) settings for roaming user profile shared folders or redirected user folders, and make sure you allow sufficient disk quotas for your users.*

11. Click Advanced in the Redirect Properties dialog box. The Advanced Security Settings For Redirect dialog box is displayed.

12. Select the Sales row and then click Edit. The Permission Entry For Redirect dialog box is displayed.

13. Select This Folder Only in the Apply Onto drop-down list. As shown in Figure 1-6, verify that the Allow checkboxes are selected for the following entries in the Permissions list box:

- Traverse Folder/Execute File

- List Folder/Read Data

- Read Attributes

- Create Folders/Append Data

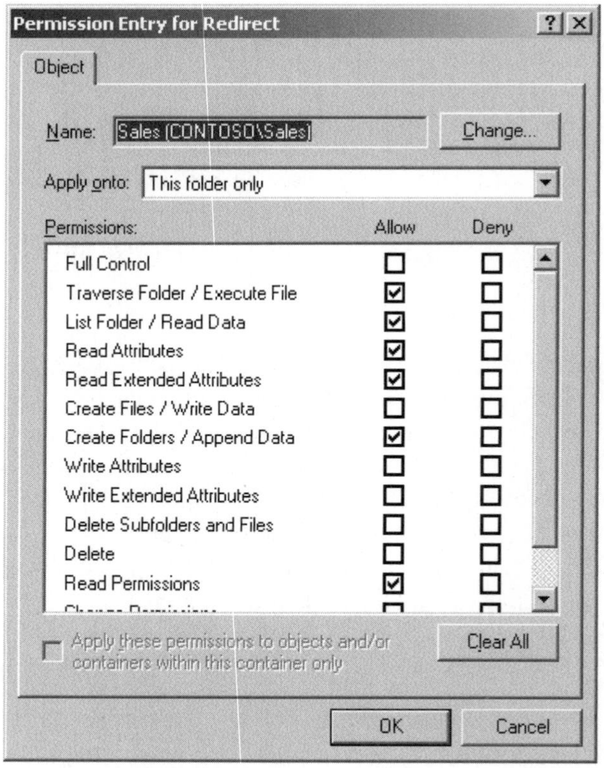

Figure 1-6
The Permission Entry For Redirect dialog box

14. Click OK to close the Permission Entry For Redirect dialog box.

15. Click OK to close the Advanced Security Settings For Redirect dialog box.

16. Repeat steps 9–15 to give the same permissions for the redirected folder to the Mktg group.

17. Click OK to close the Redirect Properties dialog box.

Question 3	*What effect does appending a dollar sign ($) to the end of a share name have?*

Exercise 1.4   Create and Link a GPO

Overview	You will create a Group Policy Object (GPO) that Windows Vista uses to administer Folder Redirection. You use GPOs to configure and manage user and computer settings on a directory-based level through an Active Directory server. For this exercise, you will create a basic GPO for Folder Redirection.
Completion time	5 minutes

1. Log on to the Windows Vista client as chrisa. (Key **contoso\chrisa** in the first box and key **p@ssw0rd** in the second box.)

2. Click Start.

3. In the Start Search text box, key **gpmc.msc** and then press Ctrl + Shift + Enter to start the Group Policy Management Console (GPMC) using administrator credentials. A User Account Control dialog box is displayed.

4. Key your administrator name and password (**netadmin** and **p@ssw0rd**). Click OK. The Group Policy Management Console is displayed.

5. In the Group Policy Management console tree, expand Forest: contoso.com>Domains>contoso.com.

6. Right-click Group Policy Objects and then select New. The New GPO dialog box is displayed.

7. In the New GPO dialog box, key **Folder Redirection GPO** in the Name text box and then click OK.

8. Right-click the contoso.com node under the Domains node and select Link An Existing GPO. The Select GPO dialog box is displayed.

9. In the Select GPO dialog box, select the Folder Redirection GPO in the Group Policy Objects list box and then click OK.

10. In the Details pane on the right, on the Linked Group Policy Objects tab shown in Figure 1-7, select the Folder Redirection GPO and then click the up arrow icon in the Details pane so that the new GPO is first in the link order hierarchy.

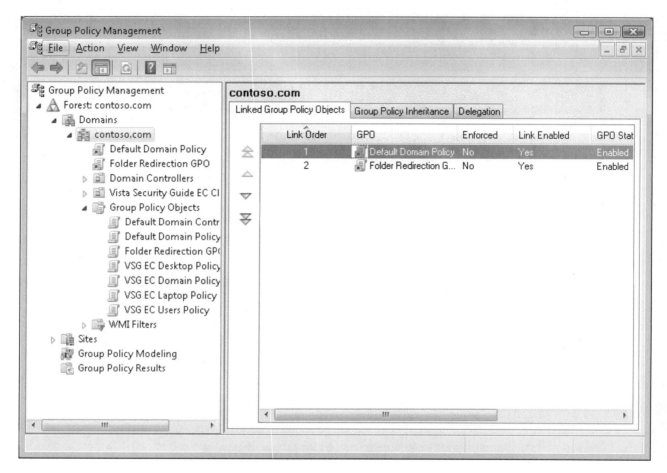

Figure 1-7
The Group Policy Management console

11. Right-click the Folder Redirection GPO in the Details pane on the right and choose the Link Enabled option if it does not already have a checkmark next to it. Click OK in the resulting Group Policy Management dialog box.

Question 4	What key combination can you press to run the Group Policy Management Console using administrator credentials when you are not logged on as an administrator?

Question 5	Why must you link the GPO?

Exercise 1.5	Configure Folder Redirection
Overview	You will establish policies that enable all users to store their desktops on a server, to share a common Pictures folder, and to store their Music folders in subfolders under their Desktop folders. Establishing this kind of folder system allows users throughout the enterprise to enjoy a predictable user experience when logged on at any physical Windows Vista client connected to the network. You can map the user experience broadly to the needs of entire departments, or you can fine-tune the user experience for smaller groups or even individual users depending on the business requirements of your enterprise.
Completion time	5 minutes

1. In the Group Policy Management console, right-click the Folder Redirection GPO link under the contoso.com node and then select Edit. The Group Policy Object Editor console is displayed.

2. In the Group Policy Object Editor console, expand User Configuration>Window Settings>Folder Redirection.

3. In the console tree, right-click the Desktop node and then select Properties, as shown in Figure 1-8. The Desktop Properties dialog box is displayed.

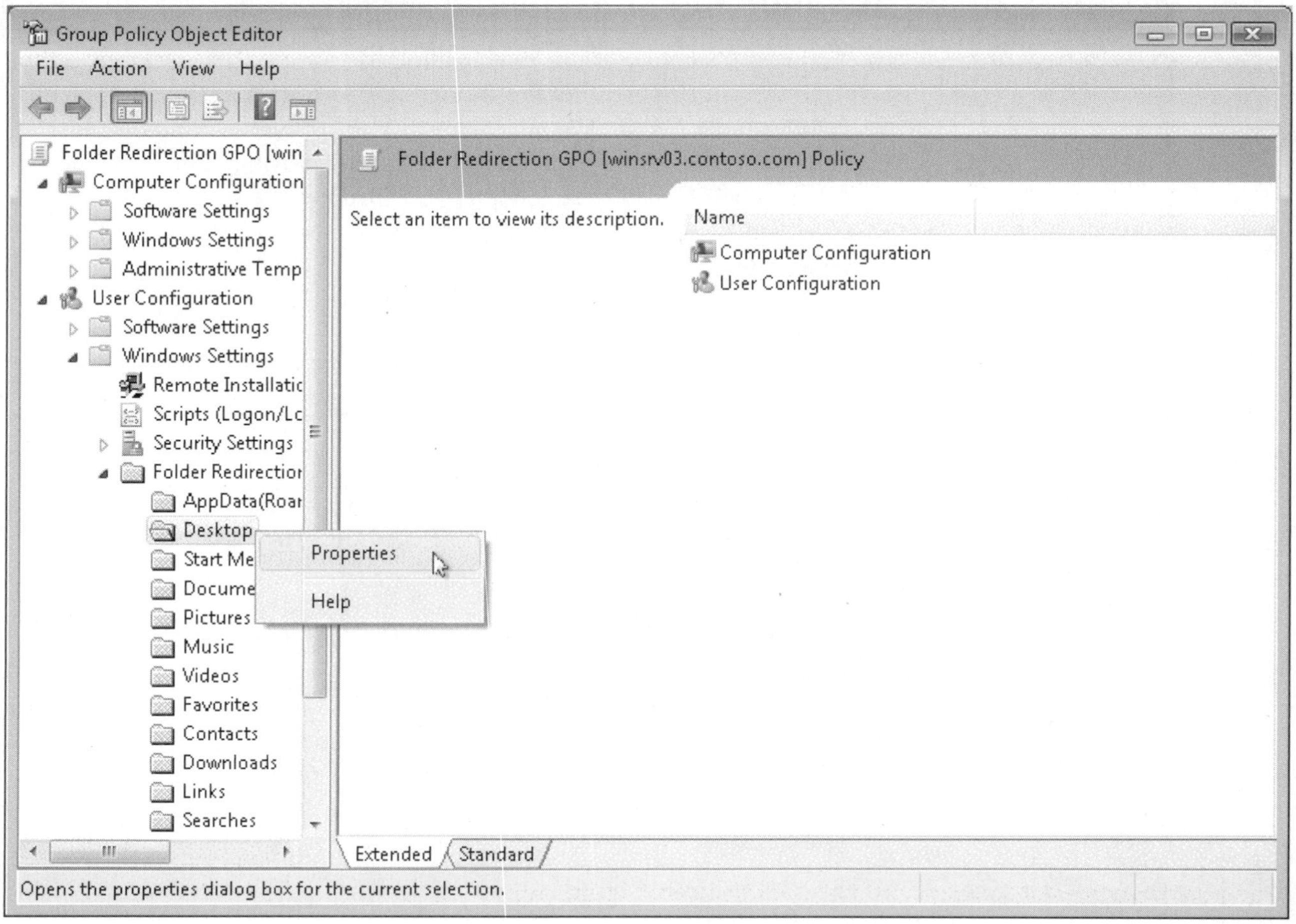

Figure 1-8
The Group Policy Object Editor console

4. On the Target tab of the Desktop Properties dialog box, select Basic – Redirect Everyone's Folder To The Same Location from the Setting drop-down list.

5. Click Browse. The Browse For Folder dialog box is displayed.

6. Browse to the following path: \\WINSRV03\Redirect\Desktops.

> **NOTE**
> *If you hid the share name by appending a dollar sign ($) to it, you must type the path manually rather than browsing to it.*

7. Select the Settings tab, change the checkboxes as shown in Figure 1-9, and then click OK.

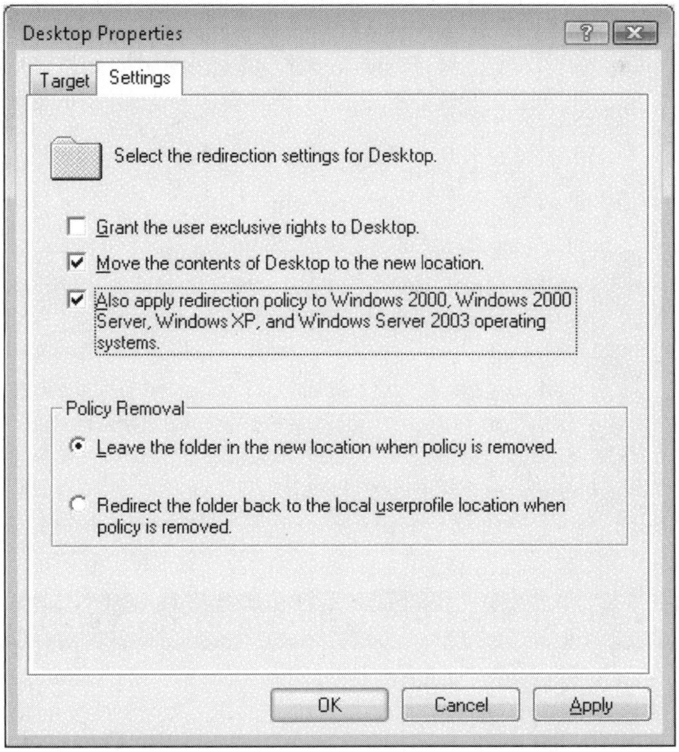

Figure 1-9
Settings for the Desktop Properties dialog box

8. In the console tree, right-click the Pictures folder and then select Properties. The Pictures Properties dialog box is displayed.

9. On the Target tab of the Pictures Properties dialog box, select Basic – Redirect Everyone's Folder To The Same Location from the Setting drop-down list.

10. Change the Target Folder Location drop-down list to Redirect To The Following Location and then set the Root Path text box to **\\WINSRV03\Redirect\Pictures**.

11. Select the Settings tab, change the checkboxes as shown in Figure 1-9, and then click OK.

12. Right-click the Music folder and then select Properties. The Music Properties dialog box is displayed.

13. On the Target tab of the Music Properties dialog box, select Follow The Documents folder from the Setting drop-down list and then click OK. A Warning box is displayed.

14. The Warning box informs you that if you have any folder's setting that is not applied to Windows 2000, 2000 Server, XP and Windows Server 2003 operating systems (OS's) you will no longer be able to change any Folder Redirection settings in this GPO from those OS's. Click Yes to continue. Each user's Music folder will then be stored as a subfolder under that user's Desktop folder. (Enterprise administrators will frequently use this setting for the Pictures and Music folders.)

15. Close the Group Policy Object Editor console.

Question 6	*In Microsoft Windows XP, what folder location corresponds to the Pictures folder in Windows Vista?*
Question 7	*What is the result of setting Folder Redirection for the Desktop node to Basic – Redirect Everyone's Folder To The Same Location? If johnt creates a file on his desktop, will sheelaw be able to see it?*

Exercise 1.6	Redirect a Folder According to Group Membership
Overview	You will create policies that cause all users in the sales department to share one common Start menu, and they will cause users in the marketing department to share a different common Start menu. This exercise demonstrates the potential for creating common user environments for employees with similar duties, tasks, and resources.
Completion time	10 minutes

1. In the Group Policy Management console, right-click the Folder Redirection GPO link under the contoso.com node and select Edit. The Group Policy Object Editor console is displayed.

2. In the Group Policy Object Editor console, expand User Configuration>Window Settings>Folder Redirection.

3. In the console tree, right-click the Start Menu folder and then select Properties. The Start Menu Properties dialog box is displayed.

4. On the Target tab of the Start Menu Properties dialog box select Advanced – Specify Locations For Various User Groups from the Setting drop-down list.

5. Click Add. The Specify Group And Location dialog box is displayed.

6. Key **Sales** in the Security Group Membership text box.

7. Change the Target Folder Location drop-down list to Redirect To The Following Location. Then set the Root Path text box to **\\WINSRV03\Redirect\Start Menus\Sales**.

8. Click OK to close the Specify Group And Location dialog box.

9. Repeat steps 5–8 for the Mktg group, setting the root path to **\\WINSRV03\Redirect\Start Menus\Mktg**.

10. Select the Settings tab, change the checkboxes as in Figure 1-9, and then click OK to close the Start Menu Properties dialog box.

11. Close the Group Policy Object Editor console.

12. From the File menu, select Exit to close the Group Policy Management console.

13. Click Start and then click the right-arrow to the right of the Search box. Click Switch User. A startup window is displayed.

14. Press Ctrl + Alt + Delete. To log on as John Tippett, key **johnt** in the User Name text box, key **p@ssw0rd** in the Password text box, and then press Enter.

15. Create a new empty text file on the Windows Vista desktop and—using Windows Explorer—create a new empty bitmap image in the Pictures folder. Name the files whatever you like. Log off of Windows Vista.

16. On the server, examine the tree structure in the Redirect share. You should find new folders for johnt in the Desktops folder, and you should also find the new files you created in step 13. You will also notice new folders in the …\Start Menus\Sales folder, but not in the …\Start Menus\Mktg folder.

17. On the server, create another new bitmap image in the Pictures folder.

18. Log back on to the client as johnt, and you should see the additional bitmap image when you browse to the Pictures folder, as shown in Figure 1-10. Notice also the Sync icons that distinguish folders and files that are stored in redirected folders and the Sync icon that is added to the taskbar.

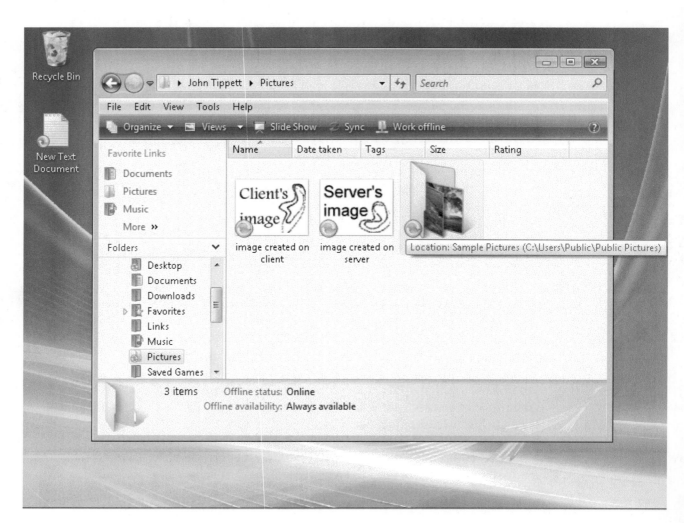

Figure 1-10
Files on the desktop and in the Pictures folder that are stored in redirected folders

19. Close any windows that remain open and log off your computer.

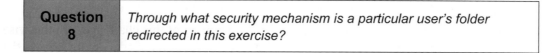

Question 8	*Through what security mechanism is a particular user's folder redirected in this exercise?*

LAB REVIEW QUESTIONS

Completion time	10 minutes

1. What tools, platforms, and logon credentials should you use to administer Group Policy Objects in a network running Windows Server 2003 and Windows Vista clients?

2. What two categories of file permission settings must you modify for users to successfully use Folder Redirection? Which specific permissions should be turned on in each category?

3. How should you secure sensitive information in profiles and redirected folders?

LAB CHALLENGE: RUN SCANSTATE AND LOADSTATE TO SAVE AND RESTORE MIGRATION DATA

Completion time	30 minutes

To practice saving and restoring user migration data, change some simple settings on the Windows Vista client, such as the background screen. Use the PrtScr key to capture an image of the desktop and save it on the server in the following location: \\winsrv03\Redirect\Pictures\prescan.bmp. (Your instructor might specify an alternate location with subfolders for each student.) Next, scan the Windows Vista client for migration data by using the Scanstate utility (as described in Lesson 1 of the textbook). You can download the USMT 3.0 install program from www.microsoft.com/downloads.

Now, change the settings you modified at the beginning of this challenge, or otherwise restore the client to its initial state. Then, re-load the scanned data by using the Loadstate utility, as if you were using the scan to migrate a user onto a fresh client. Again, use the PrtScr key to capture an image of the desktop and save it on the server in the following location: \\winsrv03\Redirect\Pictures\postscan.bmp. (Your instructor might specify an alternate location with subfolders for each student.)

LAB 2
DEPLOYING WINDOWS VISTA

This lab contains the following exercises and activities:

Exercise 2.1   Install the Windows Automated Installation Kit (WAIK)

Exercise 2.2   Create a Windows PE Boot CD

Exercise 2.3   Create and Save a Machine Image

Exercise 2.4   Boot a Fresh Machine with Windows PE

Exercise 2.5   Prepare the New Machine's Hard Drive

Exercise 2.6   Apply the Machine Image

Lab Review   Questions

Lab Challenge   Apply an ImageX Image from a CD

SCENARIO

As the network administrator for Contoso, you have already configured Microsoft Windows Vista on a machine by using installation settings that will be the company standard. You plan to replicate this standard installation throughout the enterprise. You must make an image of your standard machine and then roll out Windows Vista by applying the image to other machines.

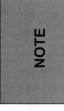

In this lab, the following terms are used:

Virtual machine. *A virtual machine running under Virtual PC.*
Host machine. *The physical machine running Virtual PC.*
Master machine. *The machine (virtual or physical) whose installation will be copied and replicated throughout an enterprise.*

After completing this lab, you will be able to:

- Create an image of a machine.

- Create and use a Windows PE boot CD.

- Format and partition a hard drive in preparation for installing Windows Vista.

- Apply a master machine image to a new machine.

- Check folder ownership.

Estimated lab time: 90 minutes

Exercise 2.1	Install the Windows Automated Installation Kit (WAIK)
Overview	The tools for creating and applying machine images are part of the Windows Automated Installation Kit, which you will need to install. To create an image, you need two tools: ImageX and a Windows PE boot CD. In this exercise, you will install the software you need to create those tools.
Completion time	5 minutes

Turn Off Folder Redirection

You will turn off the Folder Redirection established in the previous lab so that the normal Start menu options are available to all users.

1. With your server started, log on to your Windows Vista client as chrisa. (If necessary, click Switch User and then click Other User. Key **contoso\chrisa** in the User Name text box, key **p@ssw0rd** in the Password text box, and then press Enter.)

2. Click Start.

3. In the Start Search text box, key **gpmc.msc** and then press Ctrl + Shift + Enter to start the Group Policy Management console (GPMC) using administrator credentials. A User Account Control dialog box is displayed.

4. Key your administrator name and password (netadmin and p@ssw0rd). Click OK. The Group Policy Management console is displayed.

5. In the Group Policy Management console tree, expand Forest: contoso.com>Domains>contoso.com. Right-click Group Policy Objects and select New. In the New GPO dialog box, key **Folder Redirection GPO** in the Name text box and then click OK.

6. Right-click the contoso.com node under the Domains node and then select Link An Existing GPO. In the Select GPO dialog box select the Folder Redirection GPO in the Group Policy Objects list box and then click OK.

7. In the Details pane, select the contoso.com node and then click the down arrow in the Details pane so that the new GPO is second in the link order hierarchy. Right-click the Folder Redirection GPO in the Details pane and then choose Link Enabled from the context menu to remove the checkmark. In the Group Policy Management dialog box that is displayed, click OK to change the Link Enabled setting for this GPO Link.

8. Close the Group Policy Management console.

Install the WAIK

9. Your instructor will supply you with a WAIK CD or with a WAIK .iso file. Insert the WAIK CD or capture the vista_6000.16386.061101-2205-LRMAIK_EN.iso file as a virtual CD and click Open. The dialog box for capturing a virtual CD when using Virtual PC is shown in Figure 2-1.

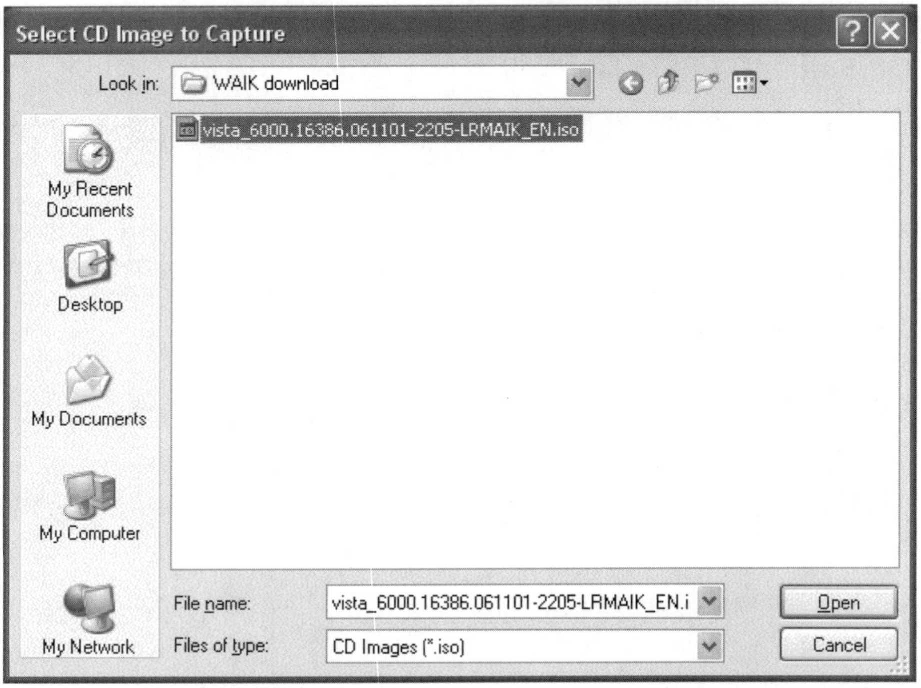

Figure 2-1
Capturing a virtual CD when using Virtual PC

You can download the WAIK from www.microsoft.com/downloads.

The Windows Automated Installation Kit (WAIK) is a 992 MB download. Depending on your lab environment, you might need to change the extension of the downloaded file from .img to .iso.

10. If the AutoPlay window is displayed, choose Run StartCD.exe. Otherwise, click Start, All Programs, Accessories, Windows Explorer. In the Folders list in the left pane, expand Computer. Then select DVD Drive (D:) WLHAIK and double-click the StartCD application.

11. In the User Account Control dialog box, provide administrator credentials (netadmin and p@ssw0rd) and then click OK.

12. In the Welcome To Windows Automated Installation Kit window shown in Figure 2-2, click Windows AIK Setup.

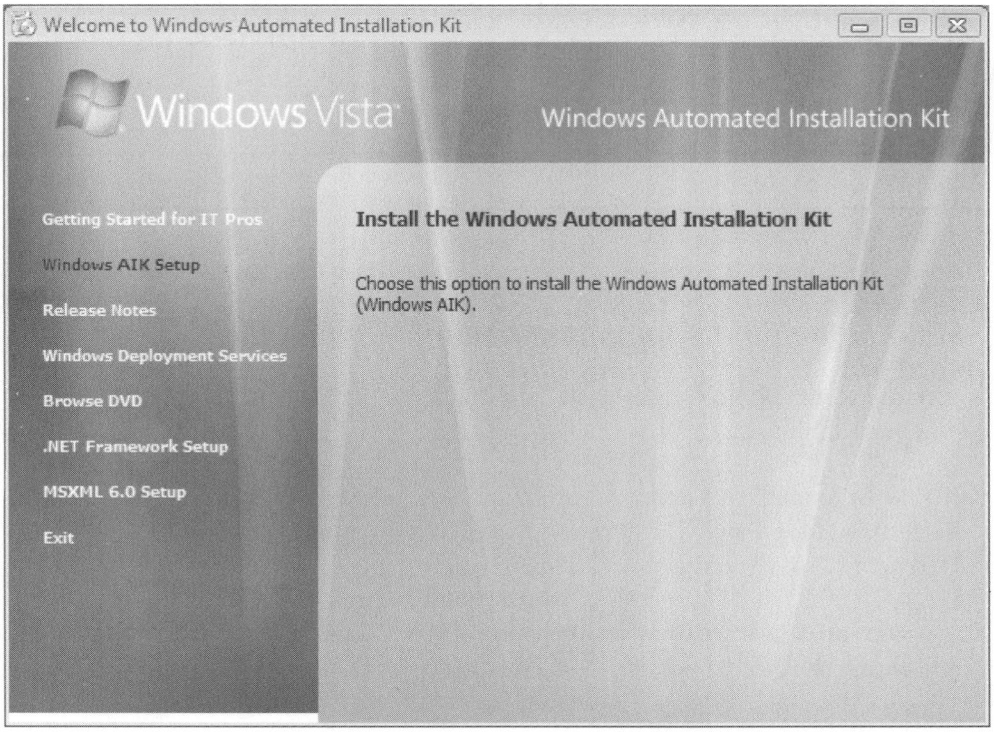

Figure 2-2
The Welcome to Windows Automated Installation Kit window

13. On the first page of the Windows Automated Installation Kit Setup Wizard, click Next. The *License Agreement* page is displayed.

14. Select the I Agree option to accept the License Agreement and then click Next. The *Select Installation Folder* page is displayed.

15. Accept the default installation location by clicking Next. The *Confirm Installation* page is displayed.

16. Click Next. The *Windows Automated Installation Kit Is Being Installed* page is displayed, containing the wizard's progress bar.

17. After the installation completes, the *Installation Complete* page is displayed. Click Close.

18. Close the Windows Automated Installation Kit window.

Exercise 2.2	Create a Windows PE Boot CD
Overview	You will use the Windows Automated Installation Kit to create a Windows PE boot CD. To use ImageX to capture an image of your master machine's operating system, you will need to boot the master machine by using Windows PE. You create a Windows PE boot CD to run this alternate operating system.
Completion time	25 minutes

1. Click Start. In the Start Search box, key **cmd** and then press Ctrl + Shift + Enter. A User Account Control dialog box is displayed.

2. Provide administrator credentials and then click OK. A command prompt window is displayed.

3. In the command prompt window, key **cd c:\program files\windows aik\tools\petools** and then press Enter. The current directory changes to C:\Program Files\Windows AIK\Tools\PETools.

4. Key **copype x86 c:\winpe** and then press Enter. This creates the Windows PE boot files in the winpe folder.

5. Key **copy "c:\program files\windows aik\tools\x86\imagex.exe" c:\winpe\iso** and then press Enter. This adds the ImageX utility to the winpe folder.

6. Key **cd c:\program files\windows aik\tools\petools** and then press Enter. The current directory changes to C:\Program Files\Windows AIK\Tools\PETools. (You can also press the up arrow until you see the command executed in step 3.)

7. Key **oscdimg -n -bc:\winpe\etfsboot.com c:\winpe\ISO c:\winpe\winpe.iso**. This creates a bootable ISO image file from the contents of the C:\winpe\ISO directory to the C:\winpe folder.

8. Burn the .iso file onto a CD. If you don't have access to a CD burner, your instructor will supply you with a CD to use in subsequent steps.

Question 1	*What must you copy to the \winpe\iso folder and why?*

> **NOTE**
>
> *If your lab environment uses Virtual PC, please note the following. Because Virtual PC does not support writing to CDs, if you are executing this procedure on a virtual machine you will need to move or copy the .iso file to the host machine to burn the .iso file onto a CD. To do so, use the Edit Settings menu on the virtual machine's menu bar. If the Note – Virtual PC dialog box is displayed warning you that some settings have been disabled, simply click OK. Select the Shared Folders item in the Setting column and then click the Share Folder button. Select a location in the host machine's file system and click OK. Click OK to close the Settings window. You can then access the shared folder as if it were a network drive. Use Window Explorer to copy the winpe.iso file to the shared folder.*

Exercise 2.3 Create and Save a Machine Image

Overview	You will run ImageX to capture an image of your master machine's Windows Vista installation directly on your master machine. Then you will copy the image to a share location on the server. You can change any of the settings or install any applications on your master machine. After you are satisfied with the setup on your master machine, you capture an image of that setup. Later you will use the image to replicate the setup on as many other machines as necessary. Note that in a real enterprise environment, you will need to follow your company's established policy regarding licensing when replicating a Windows Vista installation on multiple machines.
Completion time	5 minutes (optionally up to 50 minutes)

> **NOTE**
>
> *Typically, on your master machine you will install and configure Windows Vista, including adding or removing any Windows components and changing any appearance, security, and ease of access settings appropriate to your enterprise. You will also install any applications that all users will need.*

1. Insert the Windows PE boot CD and restart your master machine. When the machine reboots, as shown in Figure 2-3, press any key at the prompt to tell it to boot using the CD as the boot disk.

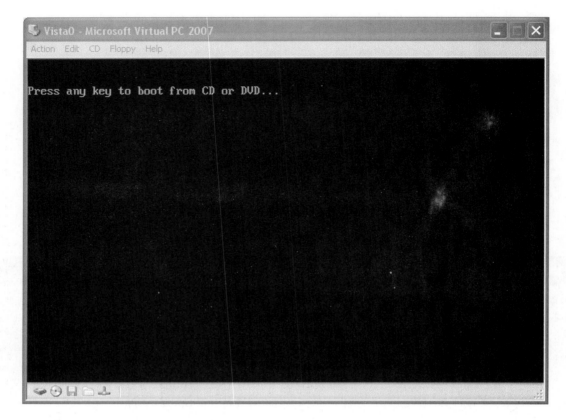

Figure 2-3
The boot prompt when restarting the machine

2. (Optional) This step can take 45 minutes or more to execute. If your instructor provides you with a vista.wim file to use in subsequent steps, you can skip this step—and possibly the rest of this exercise—depending on how the instructor supplies the vista.wim file. At the command prompt, key **d:\imagex /capture c: c:\vista.wim "vista master"** and then press Enter. This will execute ImageX from the root of drive D with the parameters identified in Table 2-1.

Table 2-1
Parameters for ImageX

Parameter	Purpose
/capture	Tells ImageX to capture an image.
c:	Tells ImageX to capture the contents at the root of drive C.
C:\vista.wim	Tells ImageX to store the captured image in a file named vista.wim at the root of drive C.
"vista master"	Tells ImageX to include this name in the captured image file. The name can be used when applying the image to extract a particular image from a file containing multiple images.

NOTE	*Although you are creating the vista.wim image file on the same drive as the drive you are capturing, this won't confuse ImageX. Later in this procedure, you will move the vista.wim file from the client to the server. Make sure, however, that the vista.wim file is deleted before you capture any subsequent image of drive C.*

After scanning the files on drive C, ImageX will present a progress indicator as shown in Figure 2-4.

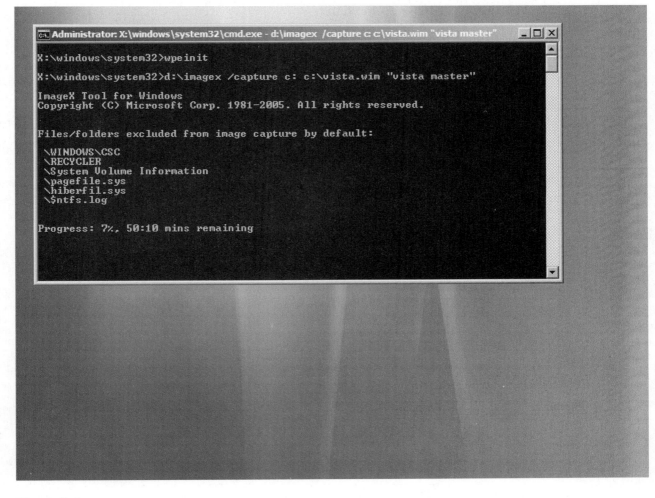

Figure 2-4
The ImageX progress indicator

> *While step 2 is executing, you can continue with steps 3–11 of this exercise, and you can complete steps 1–10 of Exercise 2.4. If you do so, don't forget to return to steps 12–17 of this exercise and then continue with step 11 of Exercise 2.4.*

3. Log on to Windows Server 2003 with your administrator account.

4. On the server, click Start, and then click Windows Explorer. The Windows Explorer window is displayed.

5. Expand the My Computer node and then select the Local Disk (C:) node.

6. Right-click in the Details pane, point to New, and then select Folder.

7. Rename the folder **Imaging**.

8. Right-click the Imaging folder and select Sharing And Security. The Imaging Properties dialog box is displayed.

9. Select Share This Folder and then click Permissions. The Permissions For Imaging dialog box is displayed.

10. The Everyone group should be selected in the Group Or User Names list box. Place a checkmark in the Allow column for the Full Control row and then click OK.

11. Click OK to close the Imaging Properties dialog box.

12. Restart the client (master) machine, allowing Windows Vista to start.

13. Log on as chrisa, as you did in Exercise 2.1.

14. Click Start, then All Programs, Accessories, and Windows Explorer. In Windows Explorer, choose Organize | Layout | Menu Bar. On the menu bar that appears, choose Tools | Map Network Drive. In the Folder list, key **winsrv03\imaging** and then click Finish.

> **NOTE**
>
> *If you are using Virtual PC, you can move the vista.wim file to a shared folder on the host machine and optionally burn it onto a CD. To move the file to the host machine, use the Edit | Settings menu on the virtual machine's menu bar. If the Note – Virtual PC dialog box appears warning you that some settings have been disabled, simply click OK. Select the Shared Folders item in the Setting column and then click the Share Folder button. Select a location in the host machine's file system and click OK. Click OK to close the Settings window. You can then access the shared folder as if it were a network drive. Use Window Explorer to move the vista.wim file to the shared folder.*

15. In the Folders list, expand Computer if necessary and select Local Disk (C:). Hold down the Shift key and drag the vista.wim file from the right pane onto the imaging (\\winsrv03) (Z:) icon to move the vista.wim file to the server.

16. Shut down the client (master) machine.

> **NOTE**
>
> *The vista.wim file is typically larger than 2 GB. You could create the file directly on the server share, but doing so takes much longer than creating it on the master machine's drive C and then moving it to the server.*

17. Log off of the server by clicking Start, clicking Log Off, and then clicking Log Off in the Log Off Windows dialog box.

> **Question 2**
>
> *In the command line **d:\imagex /capture c: c:\vista.wim "vista master"**, what are the parameters and what do they do?*

Exercise 2.4	Boot a Fresh Machine with Windows PE
Overview	You boot a new machine by using your new Windows PE boot CD. To apply an image to a new machine, the new machine must boot using a temporary operating system, Windows PE.
Completion time	5 minutes

1. Insert the Windows PE boot CD.

2. Reboot the machine.

3. When the machine reboots, press any key at the prompt to tell it to boot using the CD as the boot disk.

Exercise 2.5	Prepare the New Machine's Hard Drive
Overview	You will prepare the hard drive for applying the Windows Vista image by partitioning and formatting the hard drive and setting the active partition. Partitioning and formatting the hard drive ensures that the correct file system is installed and the drive is emptied of any previous data. (Note, however, that you can use ImageX to apply an image without disturbing existing data.)
Completion time	5 minutes

1. In the Windows PE command prompt window, key **diskpart** and then press Enter.

2. Key **select disk 0** and then press Enter.

3. Key **clean** and then press Enter.

4. Key **create partition primary** and then press Enter.

5. Key **select partition 1** and then press Enter.

6. Key **active** and then press Enter.

7. Key **format** and then press Enter.   Assign Letter = C

8. Key **exit** and then press Enter.

Question 3	*What diskpart utility steps are necessary to prepare a hard drive for installing Windows Vista by using ImageX?*

Exercise 2.6   Apply the Machine Image

Overview	You will apply the image and boot your new machine with an installation and setup that is identical to the master machine on which the image was captured.
Completion time	40 minutes

1. In the Windows PE command prompt window, key **net use y: \\winsrv03\imaging** and then press Enter.

2. You will be prompted for a user name. Key **contoso\netadmin** and then press Enter.

3. You will be prompted for a password. Key the administrator password **p@ssw0rd** and then press Enter.

4. Key **d:\imagex /apply y:\vista.wim 1 c:** and then press Enter. Ignore the Info messages that scroll by.

5. Remove the Windows PE boot CD and reboot the machine by keying **exit** and then pressing Enter.

   If you receive a message saying that Winload.exe is missing or corrupt, insert the Windows PE boot CD and then press the Esc key to reboot. Press any key while rebooting to boot from the CD. (It might take a few tries before your machine senses your keypress and enables you to boot from the CD.) Edit the boot command file as follows: At the command prompt, key **bcdedit**, press Enter, and then review the output to confirm that the device and osdevice parameters are correctly set in both the {bootmgr} and {default} (or {current}) sections. The output should look similar to Figure 2-5.

Figure 2-5
The output from bcdedit

If necessary, use the following commands to set the device and osdevice parameters. You might need to substitute the appropriate identifier for bootmgr and default and the appropriate drive letter for C: to match your configuration. At the command prompt, enter the following three commands:

```
X:\Windows\System32>bcdedit      /set      {bootmgr}      device
partition=c:
```

```
X:\Windows\System32>bcdedit      /set      {default}      device
partition=c:
```

```
X:\Windows\System32>bcdedit /set {default} osdevice partition=c:
```

Remove the Windows PE boot CD and reboot the machine by keying **exit** and then pressing Enter. Windows Vista should boot normally.

NOTE	*If you are using Virtual PC and you intend to use the new virtual machine you just set up, you will probably want to choose Action	Install or Update Virtual Machine Additions from the virtual machine menu bar.*

6.   Close your client and server machines.

LAB REVIEW QUESTIONS

Completion time	5 minutes

1. What two tools are necessary for creating and applying a Windows Vista image from a master machine to target machines? How do you create the tools?

2. What command-line utility do you use to prepare a hard drive when using ImageX to apply a Windows Vista image?

3. What are some examples of locations or media from which you can apply an ImageX image?

LAB CHALLENGE: APPLY AN IMAGEX IMAGE FROM A CD

Completion time	60 minutes

Even if you are rolling out a Windows Vista installation by using the network, occasionally you will need to install Windows Vista on a machine by using removable media such as a CD or DVD. In this scenario, you want to roll out the standard Windows Vista installation to a machine that is not connected to the network.

Burn the vista.wim file to CD as described in Exercise 2.3. Boot your target machine with the Windows PE boot CD and copy the ImageX utility to the RAM drive (X:). Remove the boot CD and insert the CD containing vista.wim. Execute ImageX from the RAM drive to apply the vista.wim image from the CD to the hard drive.

LAB 3
POST-DEPLOYMENT TASKS: DEVICES AND APPLICATIONS

This lab contains the following exercises and activities:

SCENARIO

Now that you have deployed Windows Vista on client machines in your enterprise, you will need to troubleshoot and fix any issues that appear on individual machines. These issues range from fixing settings so that a user can continue to use the hardware they have available to changing settings with the aim of enhancing an individual user's interface experience or meeting an individual's accessibility needs.

After completing this lab, you will be able to:

- Check, install, and uninstall legacy devices.

- Configure Group Policy for devices.

- Modify local screen appearance settings.

- Evaluate and set ease of access settings.

- Configure application compatibility.

Estimated lab time: 50 minutes

Exercise 3.1	Install a Modem
Overview	You will install a modem. A manager in your enterprise has a legacy modem on her machine. The modem is a 9600 bps modem. You will install the driver for the modem.
Completion time	5 minutes

1. With your server started, log on to your Windows Vista client as chrisa. (Key **contoso\chrisa** in the User name text box and key **p@ssw0rd** in the Password text box. Then press Enter.)

2. Click Start and then click Control Panel.

3. Click Hardware And Sound. The Hardware And Sound window is displayed.

4. Click Phone And Modem Options. If this is the first time you have entered the modem wizard, it prompts you for location information. Enter your area code and click OK. The Phone And Modem Options dialog box is displayed.

5. Select the Modems tab and then click Add. The User Account Control dialog box is displayed.

6. Enter your administrator credentials and then click OK. The Add Hardware Wizard is displayed.

7. Select Don't Detect My Modem; I Will Select It From A List checkbox and then click Next. The *Install New Modem* page is displayed.

8. Select (Standard Modem Types) in the Manufacturer list box and then select Standard 9600 bps Modem in the Models list box, as shown in Figure 3-1. Click Next. The *Select The Port(s) You Want To Install The Modem On* page is displayed.

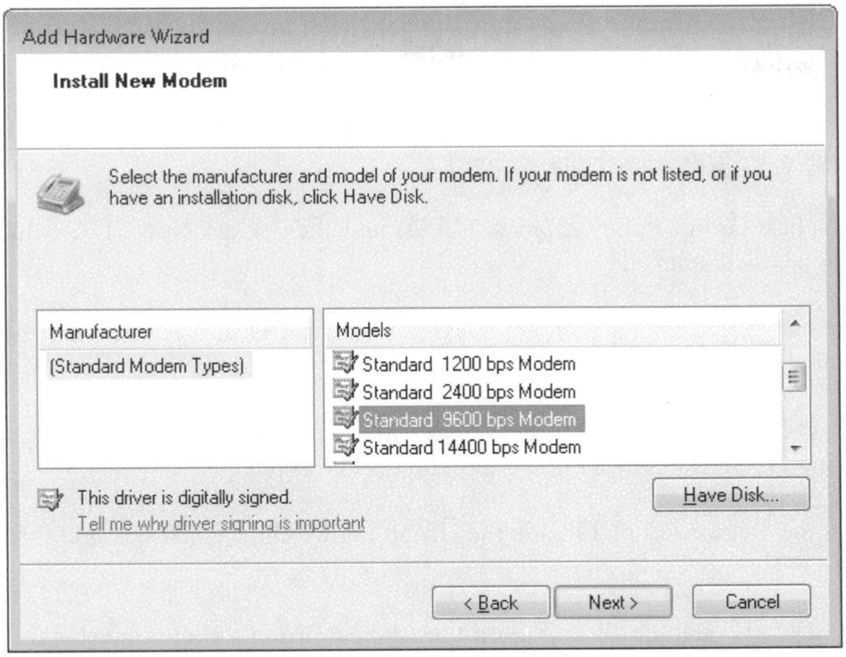

Figure 3-1
The *Install New Modem* page

9. Select the Selected ports option and then, in the list box of ports, select COM1. Click Next. Windows installs the new modem.

10. Click Finish on the *Modem Installation Is Finished* page to close the Add Hardware Wizard, click OK to close the Phone And Modem Options dialog box, then close the Control Panel.

Exercise 3.2	Configure Device Group Policy
Overview	You will configure a Group Policy for devices to turn on a screen saver for all users. To ensure that all monitors in your enterprise are protected from screen burn-in, you will turn on a screen saver for all users in the company. You want all users to have the Windows Logo screen saver activate after 5 minutes without user activity.
Completion time	10 minutes

Create a New GPO

1. Still logged on to your Windows Vista client as chrisa, click Start.

2. In the Start Search text box, key **gpmc.msc** and then press Ctrl + Shift + Enter to start the Group Policy Management console (GPMC) using administrator credentials. A User Account Control dialog box is displayed.

3. Key your administrator name and password (**netadmin** and **p@ssw0rd**). Click OK. The Group Policy Management console is displayed.

4. In the Group Policy Management console tree, expand Forest: contoso.com>Domains>contoso.com.

5. Right-click Group Policy Objects (GPO) and then select New. The New GPO dialog box is displayed.

6. In the New GPO dialog box, key **Device Policy GPO** in the Name text box and then click OK.

7. Right-click the contoso.com node under the Domains node and select Link An Existing GPO. The Select GPO dialog box is displayed.

8. Select the Device Policy GPO in the Group Policy Objects list box and then click OK.

9. In the Details pane on the right, on the Linked Group Policy Objects tab, select the Device Policy GPO and then click the up arrow in the Details pane so that the new GPO is first in the link order hierarchy.

10. Right-click the Device Policy GPO in the Details pane on the right and choose the Link Enabled option if it does not already have a checkmark next to it. Click OK in the resulting Group Policy Management dialog box.

Set the Device Policy for the New GPO

11. In the Group Policy Management console tree, right-click the Device Policy GPO link under the contoso.com node and then select Edit. The Group Policy Object Editor console is displayed.

12. In the Group Policy Object Editor console, expand User Configuration>Administrative Templates>Control Panel node. Then select the Display node. Display settings appear in the Details pane, as shown in Figure 3-2.

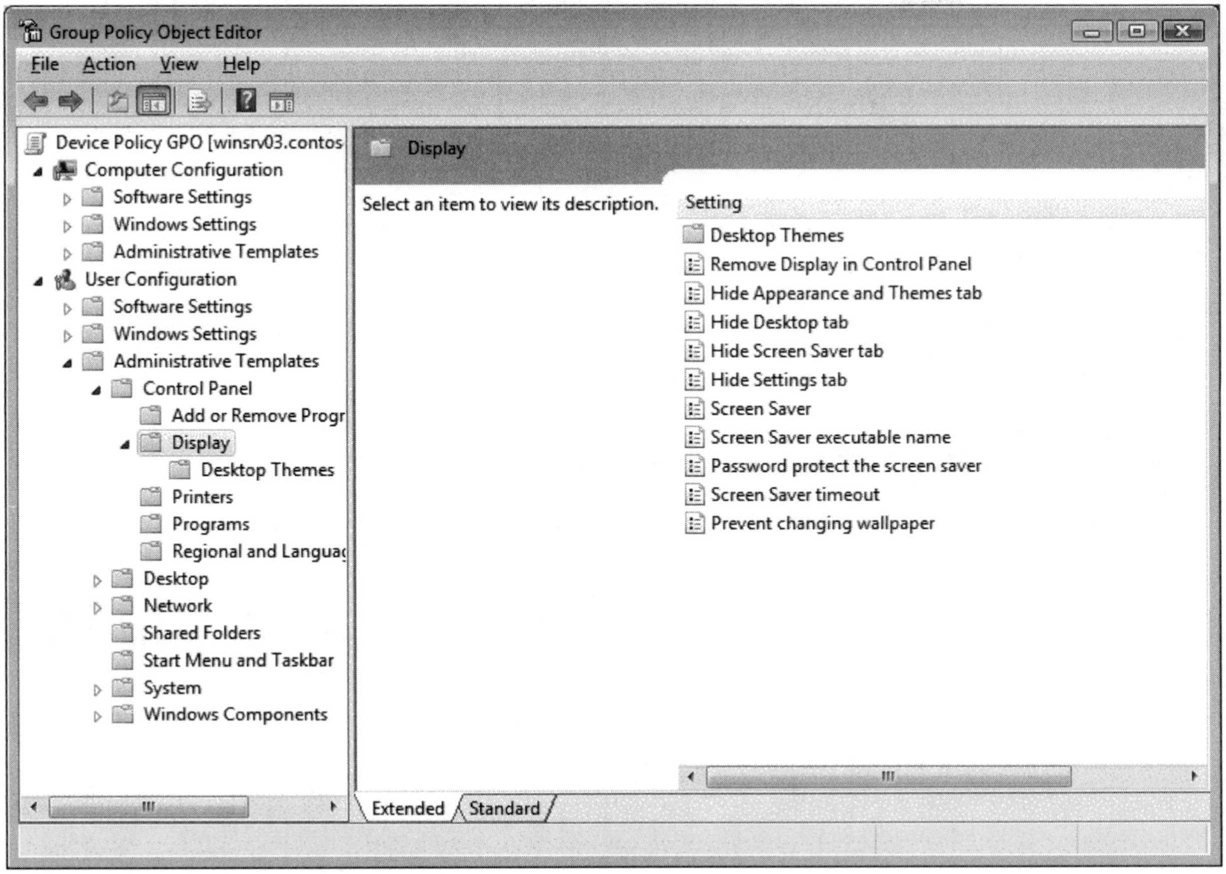

Figure 3-2
The Group Policy Object Editor console

13. In the Details pane, right-click Screen Saver and then select Properties. The Screen Saver Properties dialog box is displayed.

14. On the Setting tab, select Enabled and then click OK.

15. In the Details pane, right-click Screen Saver Executable Name and then select Properties. The Screen Saver Executable Name Properties dialog box is displayed.

16. On the Setting tab, select Enabled, key **logon.scr** in the Screen Saver Executable Name text box, and then click OK. The file name extension for screen savers is .scr, and Logon.scr is the executable name for the Windows Logo screen saver. These files are found in the \Windows\System32 folder.

17. Click OK to close the dialog box.

18. In the Details pane, right-click Screen Saver Timeout and select Properties. The Screen Saver Timeout Properties dialog box is displayed.

19. On the Setting tab of the Screen Saver Timeout Properties dialog box, select Enabled, set the Seconds to **300**, and then click OK.

20. Close the Group Policy Object Editor and the Group Policy Management consoles.

Changes you make to the Device Policy GPO won't take effect until the next time you log on.

Question 1	*After you have set a specific screen saver by using a Group Device Policy, can a user modify the screen saver?*

Exercise 3.3   Change Screen Resolution and Appearance

Overview	You will increase the screen real estate by increasing the number of pixels displayed, and you will change the wall paper. Users sometimes prefer large print on the screen, in which case they will want lower resolution settings for their screens. Others prefer to be able to see more of their applications and more within individual applications, in which case they will want higher screen resolutions. Other settings, such as text smoothing, can be modified to enhance legibility or otherwise improve screen appearance depending on an individual's esthetic tastes or physical needs.
Completion time	5 minutes

1. Still logged on as chrisa, right-click an empty area of the desktop and then select Personalize from the context menu.

2. In the Personalization Control Panel that is displayed, click Display Settings.

If you are using a virtual machine, Virtual PC changes the size of the virtual machine's window so that the resolution on the virtual machine's display matches the resolution on the host machine. You can select Action | Full Screen Mode from the virtual machine's menu bar to see the effect of various resolution settings as they would appear on an actual physical machine. To switch out of Full Screen Mode, press Right Alt + Enter.

3. In the Display Settings dialog box, drag the Resolution slider to select a resolution of 1024 by 768 pixels, as shown in Figure 3-3. Click OK.

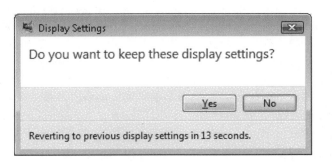

Figure 3-3
The Display Settings dialog box

4. In the Display Settings message box that is displayed, click Yes to indicate that you want to keep the new settings, as shown in Figure 3-4.

Figure 3-4
The Display Settings confirmation message box

5. In the Personalization Control Panel, click Window Color And Appearance. The Appearance Settings dialog box is displayed.

6. Click the Effects button. The Effects dialog box is displayed.

7. Clear the option labeled Use The Following Method To Smooth Edges Of Screen Fonts and click OK. Clearing this option can enhance legibility of screen elements.

8. Click OK to close the Appearance Settings dialog box. Then close the Control Panel.

Exercise 3.4	Check Ease of Access
Overview	You will review settings that Windows recommends, give specific responses to ease of access questions, then experiment with a particular ease of access setting. An individual in the enterprise has difficulty viewing the monitor. In this exercise, you will run the Ease Of Access Wizard to establish settings that will make it easier for this individual to use the Windows Vista client.
Completion time	5 minutes

1. Click Start and then click Control Panel. The Control Panel window opens.

2. Click Let Windows Suggest Settings under Ease Of Access. The Get Recommendations To Make Your Computer Easier To Use Wizard is displayed.

3. In the Eyesight (1 of 5) section, select the option labeled Images And Text On TV Are Difficult To See (Even When I'm Wearing Glasses) and the option labeled Lighting Conditions Make It Difficult To See Images On My Monitor. Then click Next.

4. In the Dexterity (2 of 5) section, leave all options unchecked and then click Next.

5. In the Hearing (3 of 5) section, select the option labeled Background Noise Makes The Computer Difficult To Hear and then click Next.

6. In the Speech (4 of 5) section, leave all options unchecked and then click Next.

7. In the Reasoning (5 of 5) section, leave all options unchecked and then click Done.

8. A list of settings that affect the conditions you selected are presented for you to configure. Review the recommended settings. Select the option labeled Turn On Magnifier and then click Apply.

9. Move your cursor around the screen, observing the results in the Magnifier pane at the top of the screen. The Magnifier is shown in Figure 3-5. Close the Magnifier dialog box, which also closes the Magnifier pane. Close the Control Panel.

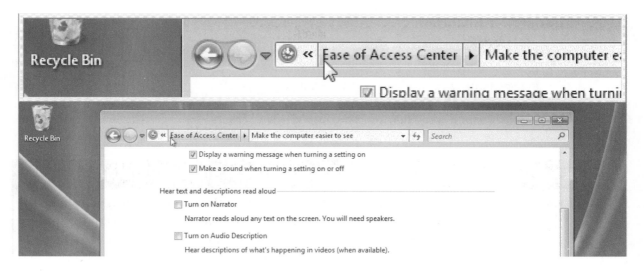

Figure 3-5
The Magnifier window at the top of the screen displays a magnified view of the screen in the vicinity of the cursor.

Question 2	*What are some of the settings that you can change to make a computer easier to use?*

Exercise 3.5	Check and Uninstall a Modem
Overview	You will check a device for any problems and then uninstall it. A manager in your enterprise has asked you to troubleshoot her department's legacy modem. After confirming that the modem is working, the manager decides to have you uninstall it anyway.
Completion time	5 minutes

Check the Modem

1. Still logged on as chrisa, click Start, right-click Computer, and then click Manage.

2. In the User Account Control dialog box, enter your administrator credentials and then click OK.

3. In the Computer Management console, click Device Manager under System Tools in the console tree.

4. In the Details pane, expand the Modems node. Check the icon for the Standard 9600 bps Modem to verify that it does not have any special flags indicating a problem.

Uninstall the Modem

5. Right-click the Standard 9600 bps Modem and then select Uninstall.

6. In the Confirm Device Uninstall warning box, click OK.

7. Close the Computer Management console.

Exercise 3.6	Configure Compatibility for an Application
Overview	You will change the application compatibility setting for an application. An employee will be using an application that must run in compatibility mode for Windows XP SP2 (Service Pack 2). You will change the compatibility mode for all users of the client machine.
Completion time	2 minutes

1. First, you will need a sample application for this exercise. If your instructor has not provided you with a sample application, download the file htmlhelp.exe from www.microsoft.com/downloads and save the file on your desktop.

The htmlhelp.exe file is an installation application. If you want, you can run htmlhelp.exe to install the HTML Help Workshop and then perform the tasks in this exercise on the application itself (hhw.exe), which is installed by default to C:\Program Files\HTML Help Workshop.

2. On your desktop, right-click the htmlhelp application and then select Properties. The htmlhelp Properties dialog box is displayed.

3. Select the Compatibility tab and then click Show Settings For All Users. A User Account Control dialog box is displayed.

4. In the User Account Control dialog box, supply your network administrator credentials (**netadmin** and **p@ssw0rd**) and then click OK. A second htmlhelp Properties dialog box is displayed with the Compatibility For All Users tab displayed.

5. On the Compatibility For All Users tab, in the Compatibility mode section, select the Run This Program In Compatibility Mode For checkbox, and then select Windows XP (Service Pack 2) from the drop-down list, as shown in Figure 3-6.

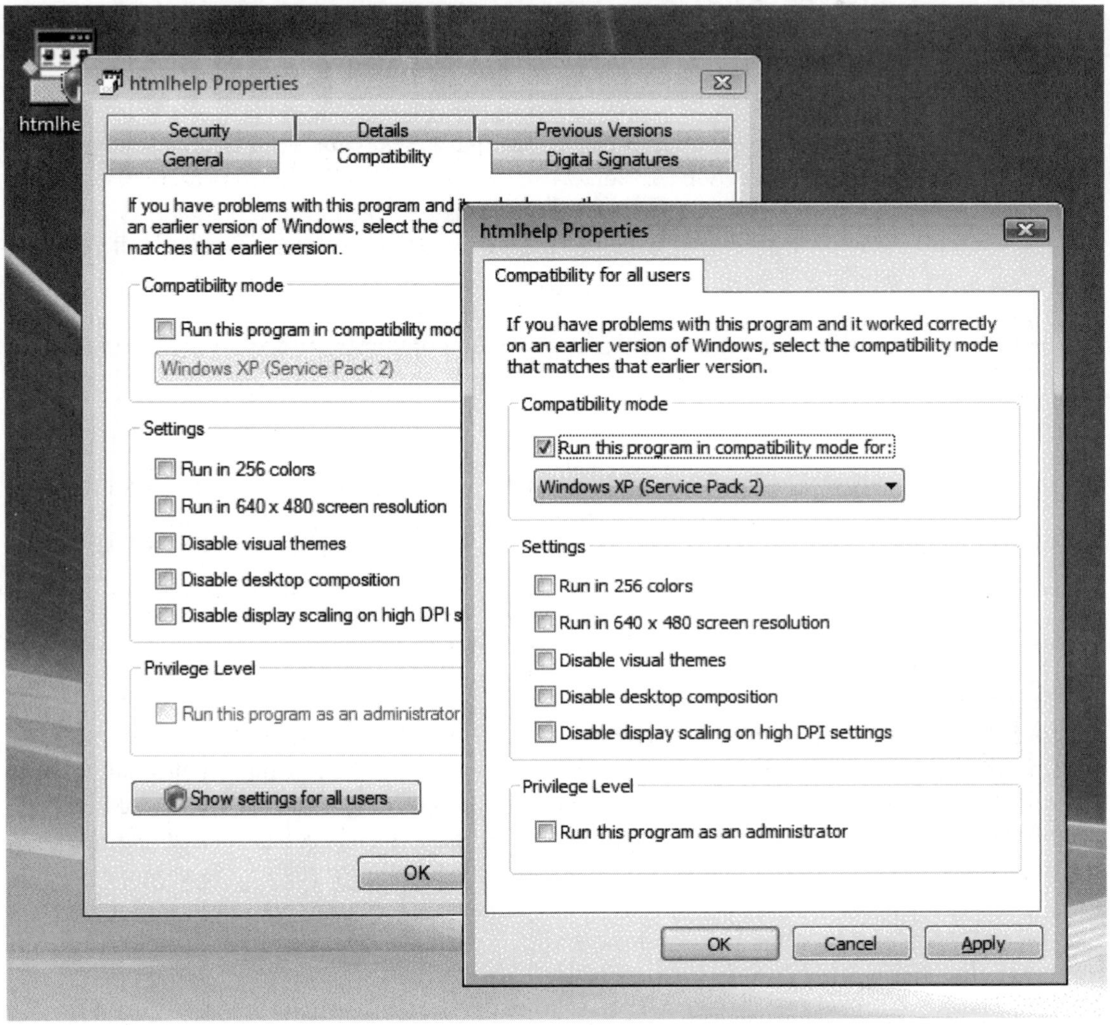

Figure 3-6
Setting an application's compatibility

6. Click OK to close the second htmlhelp Properties dialog box.

7. Click OK again to close the first htmlhelp Properties dialog box.

LAB REVIEW QUESTIONS

Completion time	10 minutes

1. To establish a device Group Policy, you must first create a GPO. How is the GPO associated with a group of users?

2. What are some of the ways in which Windows Vista's ease of access settings can enhance a user's ability to work with their computer?

3. Is there any difference when setting application compatibility for all users rather than just for the user who is currently logged on?

LAB CHALLENGE: RESTRICT DEVICES THAT USERS CAN INSTALL

Completion time	20 minutes

Create a new GPO called **Device Installation GPO** and use it to establish restrictions on what users can install. Use your GPO to implement a policy that enables administrators to install restricted devices. Create both a whitelist (for allowed applications) and a blacklist (for disallowed applications) to restrict what can be installed by users without administrator credentials. Use the PrtScr key to capture an image of the restriction lists and save the image or images on the server in \\winsrv03\Redirect\Pictures\restrictionXX.bmp. (Your instructor might specify an alternate location with subfolders for each student.)

LAB 4
USING GROUP POLICY

This lab contains the following exercises and activities:

SCENARIO

You have a basic default security policy in place but want to examine its effects on an individual client and the entire system. In particular, you want to track access to global system objects on an individual machine. After setting up the tracking, we will fast-forward, assume the tracking is complete, and turn off the local tracking. Then, you will focus on gathering information about a particular user's security settings and explore how those settings would be affected if the user switched from one user group to another. You will review the results of the proposed security change in report form and through the standard Group Policy Object Editor console interface.

After completing this lab, you will be able to:

- Set account elevation permission.

- Modify LGPO (local GPO) settings.

- Disable local Group Policy settings.

- Immediately apply GPO updates by using gpupdate.

- Use the Group Policy Results Wizard to review current Group Policy settings.

- Use the Group Policy Modeling Wizard to examine the effect of changing Group Policy settings.

- View results of the Group Policy Modeling Wizard in report form.

- View results of the Group Policy Modeling Wizard through the Group Policy Object Editor console interface.

Estimated lab time: 50 minutes

Exercise 4.1	Allow Account Elevation for Group Policy Management Console
Overview	You will allow basic users to elevate their security settings when running an application. To allow your administrative staff to log on with basic user permission and elevate their security settings only when necessary, you must establish a security environment that permits account elevation.
Completion time	5 minutes

1. With your server started, log on to your Windows Vista client as netadmin. (Key **contoso\netadmin** in the first box, key **p@ssw0rd** in the second box, and then press Enter.)

2. Click Start. In the Start Search text box, key **gpmc.msc** and press Enter. A User Account Control dialog box is displayed.

3. Provide your administrator credentials (if necessary, key **contoso\netadmin** in the User Name text box and key **p@ssw0rd** in the Password text box) and then click OK. The Group Policy Management console (GPMC) is displayed.

4. In the Group Policy Management tree, expand Forest: contoso.com>Domains>contoso.com.

5. Right-click the Default Domain Policy node and click Edit. The Group Policy Object Editor console is displayed.

6. In the Default Domain Policy tree, expand Computer Configuration>Windows Settings>Security Settings>Local Policies and select Security Options.

7. In the Details pane, scroll to find the User Account Control: Behavior Of The Elevation Prompt For Standard Users item. Right-click the item and click Properties. The User Account Control: Behavior Of The Elevation Prompt For Standard Users dialog box is displayed.

8. Verify that the Define This Policy Setting option is active and then chose Prompt For Credentials in the drop-down list. Click OK.

9. Close the Group Policy Object Editor console. Close the Group Policy Management console and log off of the client as netadmin.

Question 1	*If an administrator is not able to log on as a standard user and elevate credentials, how can the administrator run the Group Policy Management console, and why is that method undesirable?*

Exercise 4.2	Edit a Local GPO
Overview	You will change settings for the local GPO to track access to global system objects. You have decided to track the way in which users at a particular client access global system objects so that you can better understand how the client is being used. You must log on to the client and set the local GPO for that client.
Completion time	10 minutes

1. Log on to your Windows Vista client as chrisa. (Key **contoso\chrisa** in the first box, key **p@ssw0rd** in the second box, and press Enter.)

2. Click Start. In the Start Search text box, key **mmc** and then press Ctrl + Shift + Enter. A User Account Control dialog box is displayed.

3. Provide local administrator credentials (key **SALES01\locadmin** in the User Name text box and key **p@ssw0rd** in the Password text box) and then click OK. The Microsoft Management console is displayed, as shown in Figure 4-1.

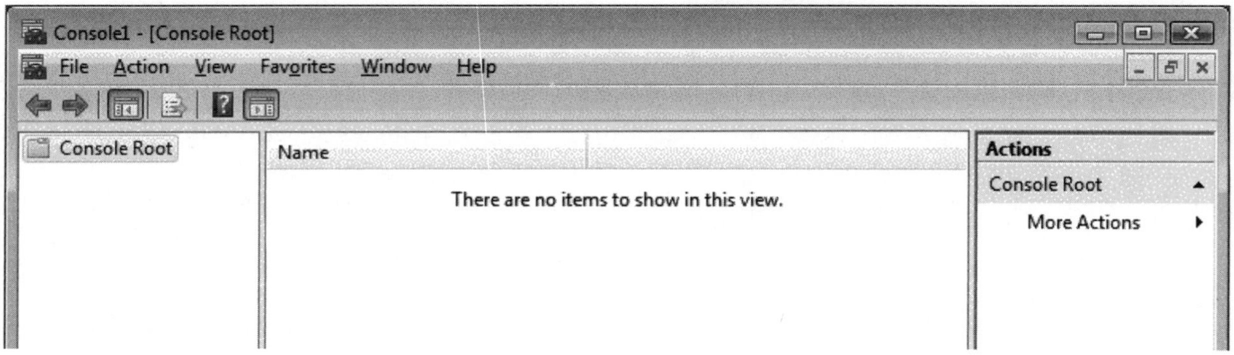

Figure 4-1
The Microsoft Management console

4. On the File menu, click Add/Remove Snap-in. The Add Or Remove Snap-ins dialog box is displayed.

5. In the Available Snap-ins list box, select Group Policy Object Editor and then click Add. The Select Group Policy Object Wizard is displayed, as shown in Figure 4-2.

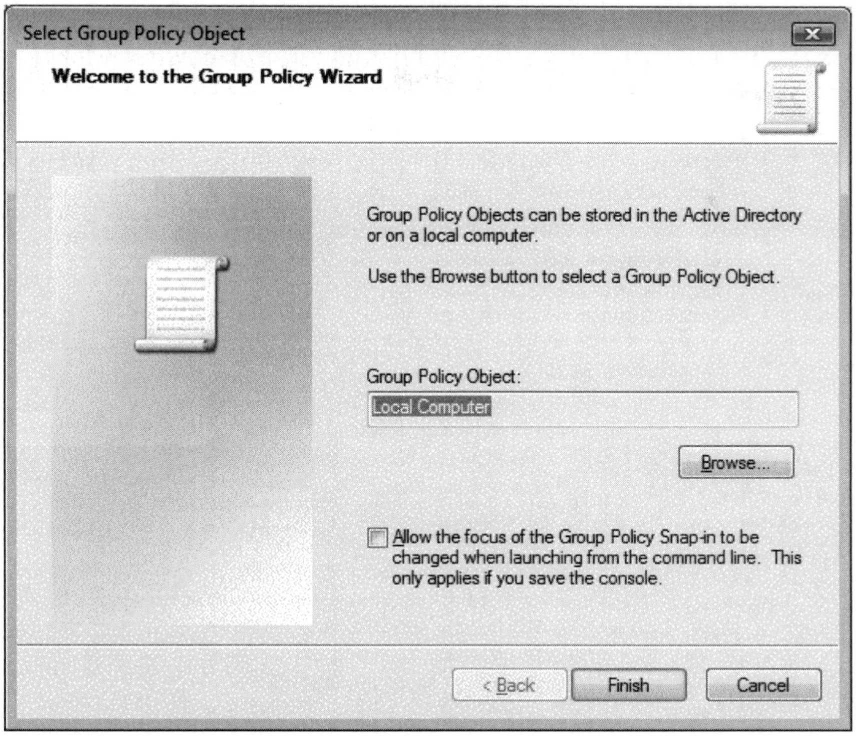

Figure 4-2
The Select Group Policy Object Wizard

6. Click Browse. The Browse For A Group Policy Object dialog box is displayed.

7. To select the local GPO (LGPO) for the computer, click the Computers tab. Verify that This Computer is selected and click OK.

8. In the Select Group Policy Object Wizard, click Finish.

9. In the Add Or Remove Snap-ins dialog box, click OK.

10. In the console tree, expand Local Computer Policy>Computer Configuration>Windows Settings>Security Settings>Local Policies. Then select Security Options.

11. In the Details pane, right-click the Audit: Audit The Access Of Global System Objects item and click Properties, as shown in Figure 4-3. The Audit: Audit The Access Of Global System Objects Properties dialog box is displayed.

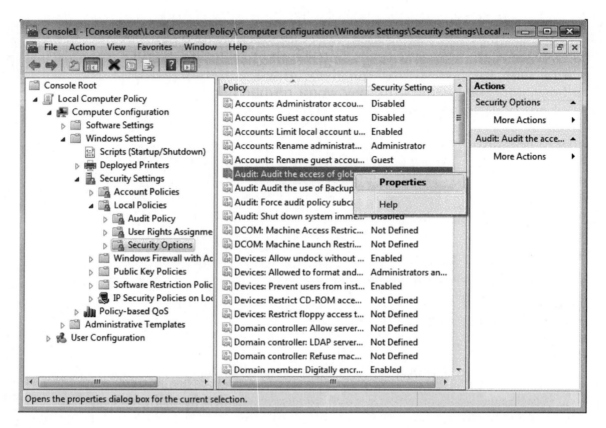

Figure 4-3
Updating an item in the Security Options node

12. Select the Enabled option and click OK.

13. Click File and then click Save as. In the Save As dialog box, key **LGPO1** in the File Name text box and click Save.

14. Close the Microsoft Management console.

Exercise 4.3	Turn off Local Group Policy
Overview	You will stop tracking global system objects by turning off local GPO processing. You will stop tracking global system objects on the local client by turning off local GPO processing. This will also ensure that the local client uses only security settings established throughout the enterprise.
Completion time	10 minutes

1. Still logged on to your Windows Vista client as chrisa, click Start.

2. In the Start Search text box, key **gpmc.msc** and then press Ctrl + Shift + Enter to start the Group Policy Management console by using administrator credentials. A User Account Control dialog box is displayed.

3. Key your administrator name and password (**netadmin** and **p@ssw0rd**). Click OK. The Group Policy Management console is displayed.

4. In the Group Policy Management console tree, expand Forest: contoso.com>Domains>contoso.com.

5. Right-click the Default Domain Policy node and choose Edit. The Group Policy Object Editor console is displayed.

6. In the Group Policy Object Editor console, expand Computer Configuration>Administrative Templates>System. Then select Group Policy.

7. In the Details pane, right-click Turn Off Local Group Policy Objects Processing and then click Properties, as shown in Figure 4-4. The Turn Off Local Group Policy Objects Processing Properties dialog box is displayed.

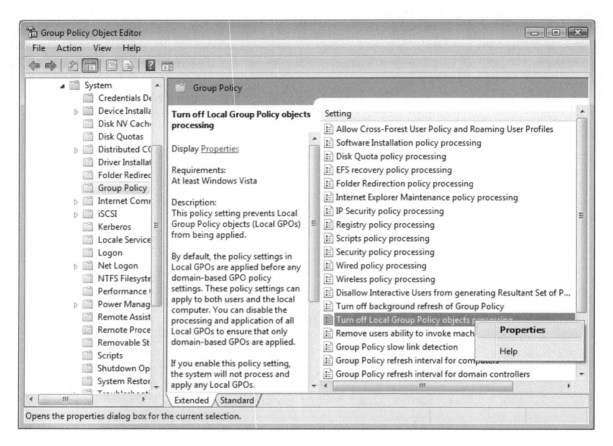

Figure 4-4
Turning off Local Group Policy objects processing

8. Select the Enabled option and then click OK.

9. Close the Group Policy Object Editor console.

10. Close the Group Policy Management console.

	What is the advantage of turning off local GPO processing rather than simply resetting the Audit: Audit The Access Of Global System Objects item to stop tracking global system objects?

Exercise 4.4	Run gpupdate to Apply New Group Policy Settings
Overview	You will run the gpupdate command-line utility. After changing security settings, you will run gpupdate to ensure that the settings take effect immediately.
Completion time	2 minutes

1. Still logged on to your Windows Vista client as chrisa, click Start. In the Start Search text box, key **cmd** and then press Enter. A command prompt window is displayed.

2. At the command prompt, key **gpupdate /force** and then press Enter. Group Policy will update as shown in Figure 4-5.

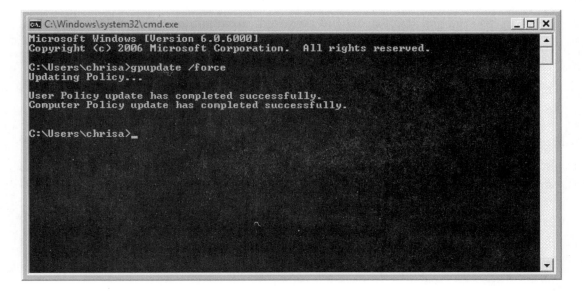

Figure 4-5
The output after running the gpupdate utility at the command prompt

3. At the command prompt, key **exit** and press Enter. The command prompt closes.

Exercise 4.5	Run the Group Policy Results Wizard
Overview	You will run the Group Policy Results Wizard to check the current security settings for a specific user. You want to see how security settings might change if a particular user switches from one user group to another. You decide to start your research by running the Group Policy Results Wizard to review and evaluate the user's current security settings.
Completion time	10 minutes

1. Still logged on to your Windows Vista client as chrisa, click Start.

2. In the Start Search text box, key **gpmc.msc** and then press Ctrl + Shift + Enter to start the Group Policy Management console using administrator credentials. A User Account Control dialog box is displayed.

3. Key your administrator name and password (**netadmin** and **p@ssw0rd**). Click OK. The Group Policy Management console is displayed.

4. In the Group Policy Management console tree, expand Forest: contoso.com, right-click Group Policy Results, and then click Group Policy Results Wizard, as shown in Figure 4-6. The Group Policy Results Wizard is displayed.

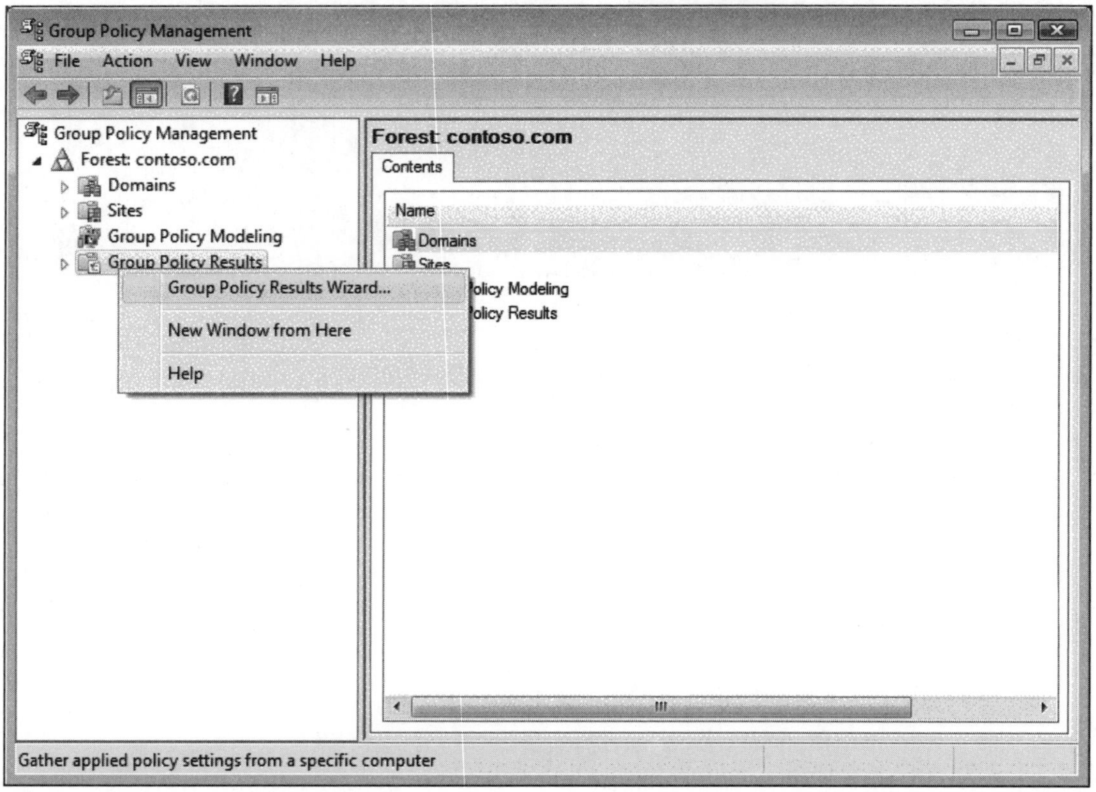

Figure 4-6
Starting the Group Policy Results Wizard

5   Click Next. The *Computer Selection* page is displayed.

6.   Select This Computer to use the local computer to generate Group Policy Results data.

7.   Click Next. The *User Selection* page is displayed.

> *For the user johnt to appear in the Select A Specific User list box on the User Selection page, you must have logged on to the client at least once as johnt.*

8.   Select the Select A Specific User option, select CONTOSO\johnt in the Select A Specific User list box. Click Next. The *Summary Of Selections* page is displayed.

9.   Ensure that the selections are correct and then click Next. The *Completing The Group Policy Results Wizard* page is displayed.

10. Click Finish. A node representing the query is displayed in the console tree under Group Policy Results, with details in the Details pane. Click the Show All link on the Summary tab in the Details pane to expand the report, as shown in Figure 4-7, and then scroll through the report to examine the summary list of security settings.

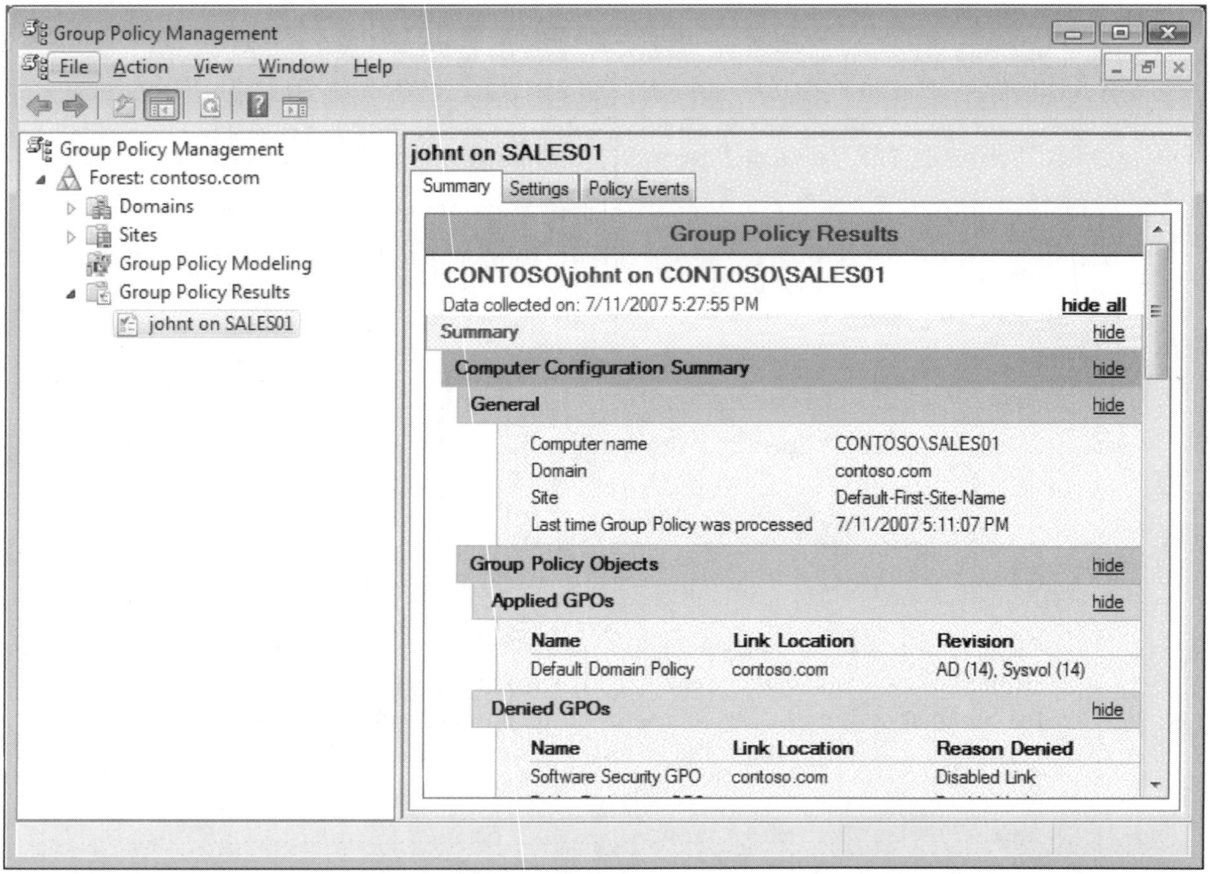

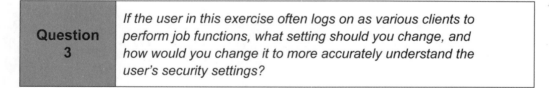

Figure 4-7
A report from the Group Policy Results Wizard

11. Close the Group Policy Management console.

Question 3	*If the user in this exercise often logs on as various clients to perform job functions, what setting should you change, and how would you change it to more accurately understand the user's security settings?*

Exercise 4.6	Run the Group Policy Modeling Wizard
Overview	You will model group policy changes by using the Group Policy Modeling Wizard. Now that you have reviewed the user's existing security settings, you will examine the settings that would be in effect if the user were to switch user groups. The Group Policy Modeling Wizard will present the results of this query in report form. In the subsequent exercise, you will review the modeling results through the Group Policy Object Editor console interface.
Completion time	10 minutes

1. Still logged on to your Windows Vista client as chrisa, click Start.

2. In the Start Search text box, key **gpmc.msc** and then press Ctrl + Shift + Enter to start the Group Policy Management console using administrator credentials. A User Account Control dialog box is displayed.

3. Key your administrator name and password (**netadmin** and **p@ssw0rd**). Click OK. The Group Policy Management console is displayed.

4. In the Group Policy Management console tree, expand Forest: contoso.com, right-click Group Policy Modeling, and then click Group Policy Modeling Wizard, as shown in Figure 4-8. The Group Policy Modeling Wizard is displayed.

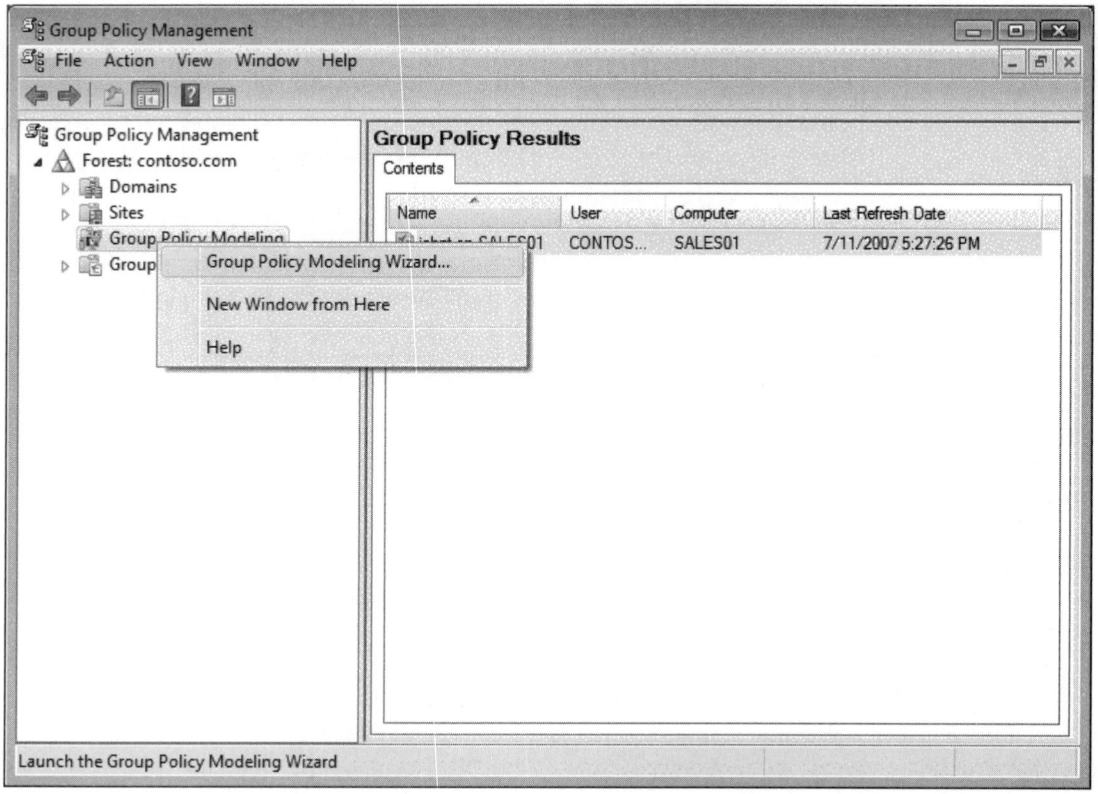

Figure 4-8
Starting the Group Policy Modeling Wizard

5. Click Next. The *Domain Controller Selection* page is displayed.

6. Click Next. The *User And Computer Selection* page is displayed.

7. In the User information section, select User and click the corresponding Browse button. The Select User dialog box is displayed.

8. In the Select User dialog box, key **johnt** in the Enter The Object Name To Select (Examples) box, as shown in Figure 4-9. Click Check Names and then click OK.

Figure 4-9
The Select User dialog box after keying johnt and clicking Check Names

9. In the Computer information section, select Container and click the corresponding Browse button. The Choose Computer Container dialog box is displayed.

10. In the Choose Computer Container dialog box, expand the contoso node, select the Computers node, and then click OK. The *User And Computer Selection* page is displayed, as shown in Figure 4-10.

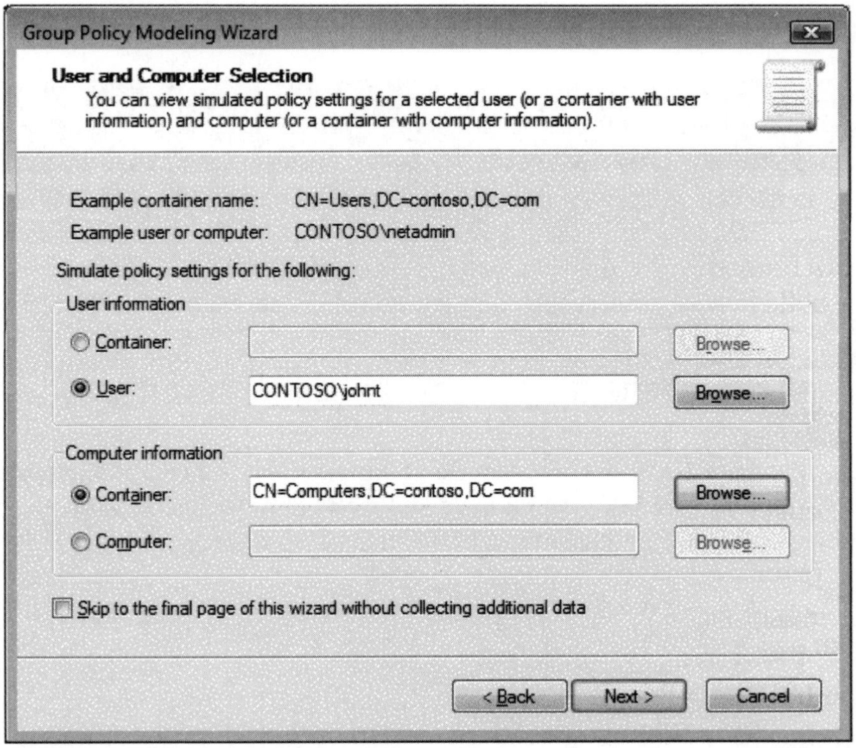

Figure 4-10
The *User And Computer Selection* page of the Group Policy Modeling Wizard

11. Click Next. The *Advanced Simulation Options* page is displayed.

12. Click Next. The *Alternate Active Directory Paths* page is displayed.

13. Click Next. The *User Security Groups* page is displayed.

14. Select CONTOSO\Sales, click Remove, and then click Add. The Select Groups dialog box is displayed.

15. In the Select Groups dialog box, key **mktg**, click Check Names, and then click OK. This allows you to model the security settings if johnt is moved from the Sales user group to the Mktg user group.

16. Select the Skip To The Final Page Of The Wizard Without Collecting Additional Data checkbox and click Next. The *Summary of Selections* page is displayed.

17. Review your selections and then click Next. The *Completing The Group Policy Modeling Wizard* page is displayed.

18. Click Finish. A report based on a model of the new Group Policy is displayed in the console tree under Group Policy Modeling, with details in the Details pane. Click the Show All link of the Summary tab in the Details pane to expand the report. Then scroll through the report to examine the summary list of security settings.

Exercise 4.7	View Group Policy Modeling Data in the RSoP Snap-In
Overview	You will review the results of the Group Policy Modeling Wizard by using the Resultant Set of Policy (RSoP) Snap-in. If you are used to looking at security settings through the Group Policy Object Editor console, reviewing security settings through the console rather than a report can be helpful.
Completion time	5 minutes

1. Continuing from the previous exercise, right-click the Johnt On Contoso node under the Group Policy Modeling node and then click Advanced View, as shown in Figure 4-11. The Resultant Set of Policy Snap-in is displayed.

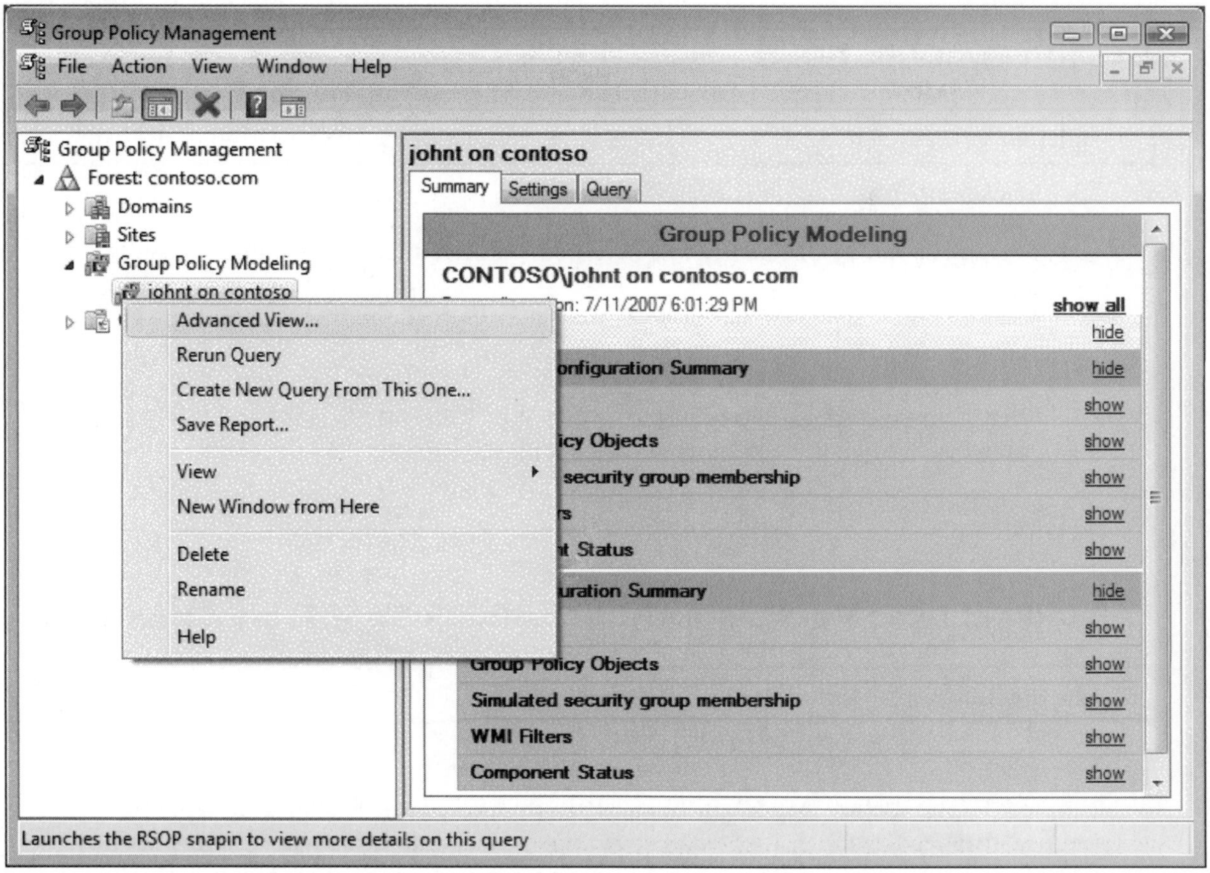

Figure 4-11
Selecting the Advanced View for a domain user

2. You can browse the console tree just like you would browse a GPO in the Group Policy Object Editor console.

3. Close the Resultant Set of Policy console and the Group Policy Management console.

LAB REVIEW QUESTIONS

Completion time	10 minutes

1. What must you do differently to edit a local GPO as opposed to a domain GPO?

2. After making changes to Group Policy, what can you do to make them take effect immediately?

3. What is the difference between the Group Policy Results Wizard and the Group Policy Modeling Wizard? In what way are they similar?

LAB CHALLENGE: MODEL ADDITIONAL SECURITY SETTING CHANGES

Completion time	10 minutes

Run the Group Policy Modeling Wizard as in Exercise 4.6, choosing your own security changes to model. List the changes you model and then review the results by using the report form and RSoP. Identify which form of review you prefer and why. List any results of the modeling that surprised you. If there were no surprises, list the results you expected and then confirmed during your review.

LAB 5
WINDOWS INTERNET EXPLORER 7 SECURITY

This lab contains the following exercises and activities:

Exercise 5.1   Turn on Internet Explorer Protected Mode Through Group Policy

Exercise 5.2   Set ActiveX Opt-In Policy

Exercise 5.3   Turn on ActiveX Installer Service

Exercise 5.4   Manage Internet Explorer Add-Ons

Exercise 5.5   Configure the Phishing Filter Through Group Policy

Lab Review   Questions

Lab Challenge   Examine Internet Explorer Settings Locally

SCENARIO

To protect clients across the enterprise from online attack, you have decided to implement a series of policies to ensure a high level of Internet security for all users. You want to establish security settings and prevent individual users from lowering security locally. To accomplish this, you will use group policies.

After completing this lab, you will be able to:

- Configure Internet Explorer Protected Mode through group policies.

- Configure ActiveX Opt-In Policy.

- Configure the ActiveX Installer Service.

- Manage Internet Explorer add-ons.

- Configure the Phishing Filter through group policies.

Estimated lab time: 60 minutes

Exercise 5.1	Turn on Internet Explorer Protected Mode Through Group Policy
Overview	You will turn on Internet Explorer Protected Mode for all users, and you will prevent individual users from turning Protected Mode off locally. You have decided to turn on Internet Explorer Protected Mode for all users to prevent websites from unexpectedly installing or running software on a client in your enterprise. Protected Mode enables Internet Explorer to browse the Internet but prompts the user if a website tries to install a program or modify system data on the client. Implementing this policy by using a Group Policy Object (GPO) prevents individual users from relaxing security constraints on any particular machine. You will leave Protected Mode turned off for the Trusted Sites and the Local Machine security zones.
Completion time	10 minutes

1. With your server started, log on to your Windows Vista client as chrisa. (If the log-on screen displays contoso\chrisa, you can simply key **p@ssw0rd** in the password box and then press Enter.)

2. Create a new GPO as instructed in Exercise 3.2, naming the new GPO **Internet Explorer 7 GPO**. Make sure the new GPO is linked and enabled as instructed in Exercise 3.2.

3. In the Group Policy Management console, right-click the Internet Explorer 7 GPO link under the contoso.com node and then select Edit. The Group Policy Object Editor console is displayed.

4. In the Group Policy Object Editor console, expand Computer Configuration>Administrative Templates>Windows Components>Internet Explorer>Internet Control Panel>Security Page. Then select the Internet Zone node. Display settings appear in the Details pane.

5. In the Details pane, right-click Turn On Protected Mode and then select Properties. The Turn On Protected Mode Properties dialog box is displayed, as shown in Figure 5-1.

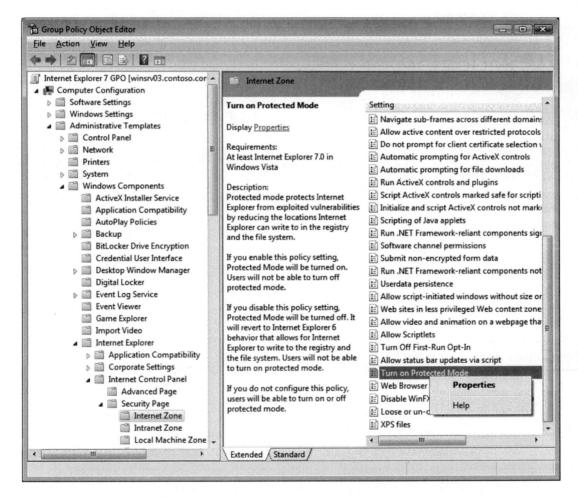

Figure 5-1
Setting the Turn On Protected Mode property

6. On the Setting tab, select Enabled and click OK.

7. In the Group Policy Object Editor console, select Intranet Zone in the console tree. In the Details pane, right-click Turn On Protected Mode and then select Properties. The Turn On Protected Mode Properties dialog box is displayed.

8. On the Setting tab, select Enabled and then click OK.

9. In the Group Policy Object Editor console, select Restricted Sites Zone in the console tree. In the Details pane, right-click Turn On Protected Mode and then select Properties. The Turn On Protected Mode Properties dialog box is displayed.

10. On the Setting tab, select Enabled and then click OK. Leave the console tree expanded in its current state and proceed to the next exercise.

 NOTE | *Changes in the Internet Explorer 7 GPO policies will not take effect until the next time you log on.*

Exercise 5.2	**Set ActiveX Opt-In Policy**
Overview	You will implement a policy forcing users to approve new ActiveX controls before installing or running them on Internet Explorer 7. You want all users to be prompted the first time an ActiveX control is run on Internet Explorer 7. The first step is to disable the Turn Off First-Run Opt-In property, which will prevent users from turning on this option locally. In the next exercise, you will add an approved installation site for ActiveX controls so that users will be prompted only when potentially harmful ActiveX controls might be run.
Completion time	10 minutes

1. Continuing from the previous exercise, in the Group Policy Object Editor console the Computer Configuration>Administrative Templates>Windows Components>Internet Explorer>Internet Control Panel>Security Page nodes should still be expanded. Select the Internet Zone node. Display settings appear in the Details pane.

2. In the Details pane, right-click Turn Off First-Run Opt-In and then select Properties. The Turn Off First-Run Opt-In Properties dialog box is displayed, as shown in Figure 5-2.

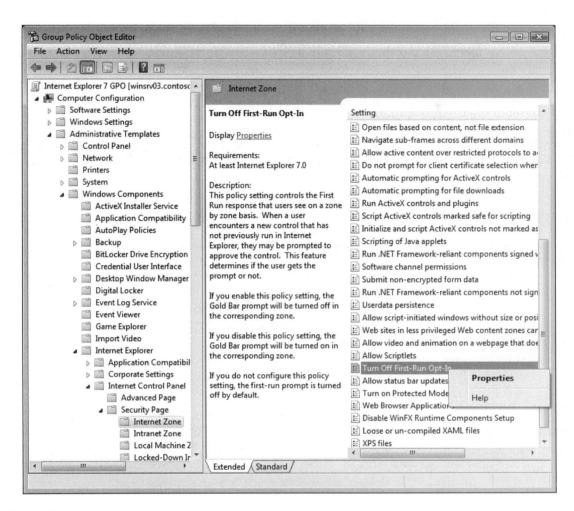

Figure 5-2
Setting the Turn Off First-Run Opt-In property

3. On the Setting tab, select Disabled (not Enabled) and then click OK.

4. In the Group Policy Object Editor console, select Intranet Zone in the console tree. In the Details pane, right-click Turn Off First-Run Opt-In and then select Properties. The Turn Off First-Run Opt-In Properties dialog box is displayed.

5. On the Setting tab, select Disabled and then click OK.

6. In the Group Policy Object Editor console, select Restricted Sites Zone in the console tree. In the Details pane, right-click Turn Off First-Run Opt-In and then select Properties. The Turn Off First-Run Opt-In Properties dialog box is displayed.

7. On the Setting tab of the Turn Off First-Run Opt-In Properties dialog box, select Disabled and then click OK. Leave the Group Policy Object Editor console open and proceed to the next exercise.

Exercise 5.3	Turn on ActiveX Installer Service
Overview	You will turn on and configure the ActiveX Installer service. To let pre-approved ActiveX controls install silently, you will establish a site from which ActiveX controls can be installed without requiring user interaction.
Completion time	10 minutes

1. Continuing from the previous exercise, in the Group Policy Object Editor console, expand the Computer Configuration>Administrative Templates>Windows Components nodes. Select the ActiveX Installer Service node. Display settings appear in the Details pane, as shown in Figure 5-3.

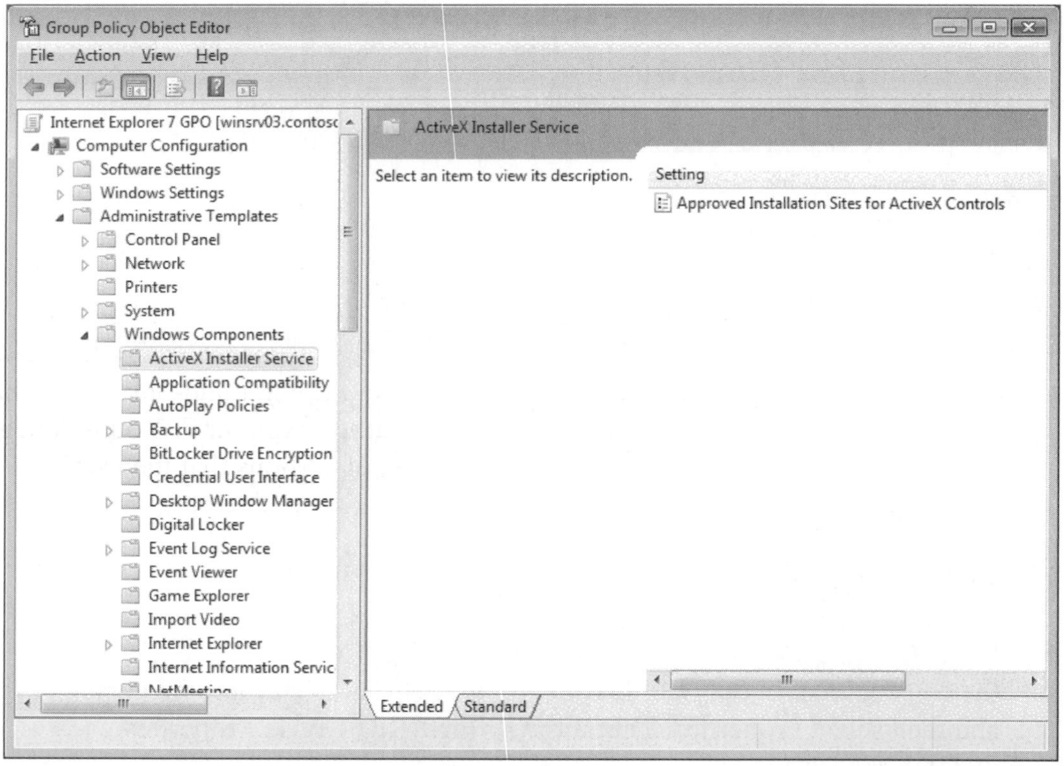

Figure 5-3
The ActiveX Installer Service node in the Group Policy Object Editor console

2. In the Details pane, right-click Approved Installation Sites For ActiveX Controls and then select Properties. The Approved Installation Sites for ActiveX Controls Properties dialog box is displayed.

3. On the Setting tab, select Enabled and then click Show. The Show Contents dialog box is displayed.

4. Click Add to add a host URL. The Add Item dialog box is displayed.

5. Key **http:\\activex.contoso.com** in the Enter The Name Of The Item To Be Added text box. Because you are certain that ActiveX controls at that location are safe, key **2,2,2,0x100** in the Enter The Value Of The Item To Be Added text box. (This sequence indicates silent installation for TPSSigned, Signed, and Unsigned controls, and that the installer should accept unknown Certificate Authorities.) This enables Internet Explorer to install ActiveX controls from that location without prompting the user. Click OK.

6. In the Show Contents dialog box, click OK.

7. In the Approved Installation Sites For ActiveX Controls Properties dialog box, click OK.

8. Do not close the Group Policy Object Editor console.

Question 1	*What do the individual components of the value 2,2,2,0x100 indicate when you add a site to the list of approved installation sites for ActiveX controls?*

Exercise 5.4	Manage Internet Explorer Add-Ons
Overview	You will delete any suspicious Internet Explorer add-ons. A user has reported problems browsing with Internet Explorer 7. You will begin troubleshooting by examining the list of add-ons that the user's installation of Internet Explorer has run and deleting any suspicious add-ons.
Completion time	10 minutes

1. Click Start, Internet. Internet Explorer is displayed.

2. From the Tools menu, select Internet Options. The Internet Options dialog box is displayed.

3. Select the Programs tab and then click the Manage Add-ons button. The
    Manage Add-ons dialog box is displayed, as shown in Figure 5-4.

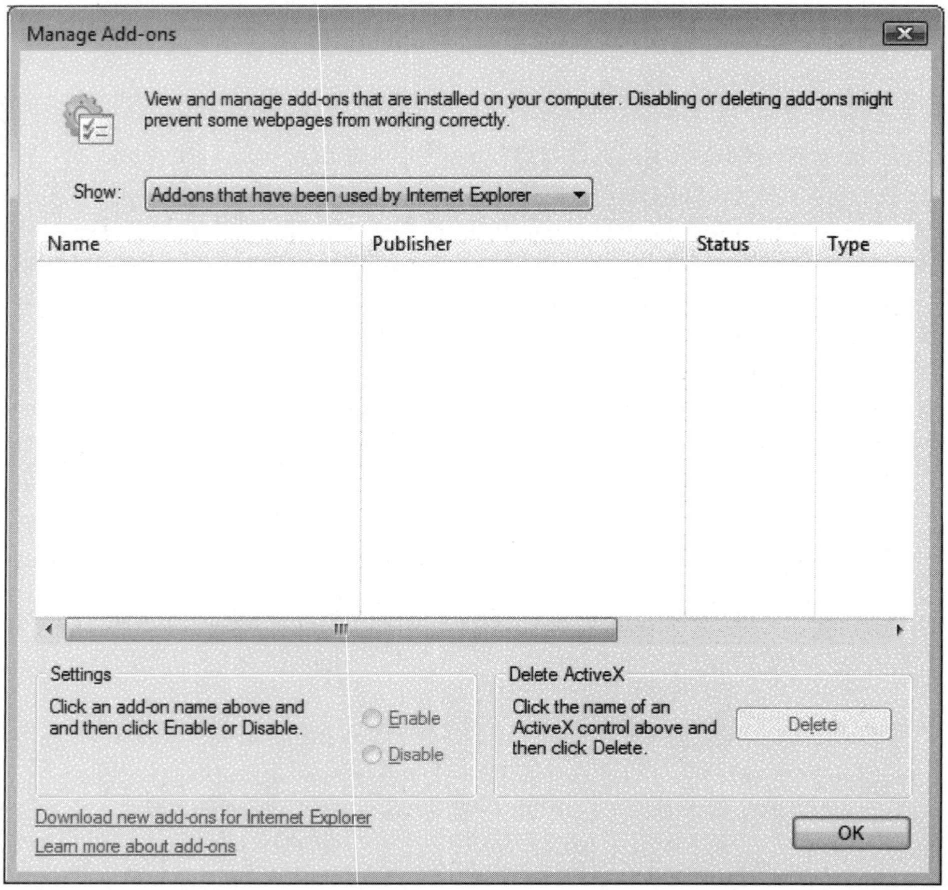

Figure 5-4
The Manage Add-ons dialog box

4. In the Show drop-down list, select Add-ons That Have Been Used By
    Internet Explorer.

If you have used Internet Explorer infrequently on your client, the list of add-ons might be empty.

5. Review the list box of add-ons. Select any that appear unusual (e.g., if you
    don't recognize the name of the publisher) and select Disable or click the
    Delete button. (Of course in a real-life environment, you would want to
    research an add-on before disabling or deleting it in case one of your end
    users requires the add-on.) When finished, click OK.

6. Click OK to close the Internet Options dialog box.

7. Close Internet Explorer.

Exercise 5.5	Configure the Phishing Filter Through Group Policy
Overview	You will turn on the phishing filter for all users. You have decided to turn on the phishing filter and to automatically send Microsoft any data that has been analyzed locally. (The phishing filter monitors websites and alerts you when it suspects that you have encountered a phishing website.)
Completion time	10 minutes

1. The Group Policy Object Editor console should still be open. Expand the Computer Configuration>Administrative Templates>Windows Components nodes. Select the Internet Explorer node. Display settings appear in the Details pane.

2. To sort the settings alphabetically, in the Details pane, click the Setting heading above the list of settings. Scroll to find the Turn Off Mananging Phishing Filter setting, right-click it, then select Properties. The Turn off Mananging Phishing Filter Properties dialog box is displayed.

3. On the Setting tab, select Enabled. Select Automatic in the Select Phishing Filter Mode drop-down list. Click OK.

4. Close the Group Policy Object Editor console.

5. Close the Group Policy Management console.

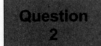 *How does the phishing filter protect users?*

LAB REVIEW QUESTIONS

Completion time	10 minutes

1. Beyond simply saving you time because you don't have to update settings on individual machines, what is the advantage in an enterprise of setting Internet Explorer security options through a GPO instead of locally?

2. How can you allow users to change Protected Mode settings according to their own preferences in any given zone?

3. What are some security settings that you can set through Group Policy that apply to specific zones? What are some security settings that apply to all zones?

LAB CHALLENGE: EXAMINE INTERNET EXPLORER SETTINGS LOCALLY

Completion time	15 minutes

Log off of the client and log back on as chrisa. Examine the security settings that you set in this lab locally. Use the PrtScr key to capture screenshots of the four settings in the following list and save the screenshots in the \\winsrv03\Redirect\Pictures folder as IEsettings1.bmp, IEsettings2.bmp, and so on. (Your instructor might have you save your screenshots in an alternate location, possibly with a subfolder for each student.)

- Restricted Sites, Protected Mode (use the Tools>Internet Options menu to view this setting)

- Restricted Sites, ActiveX controls and plug-ins, Allow previously unused ActiveX controls to run without prompt (click the Custom Level button from the Security tab of the Internet Options dialog box to view this setting)

- Restricted Sites, Miscellaneous, UsePhishing Filter (click the Custom Level button from the Security tab of the Internet Options dialog box to view this setting)

- ActiveX Installer Service (use Control Panel>Programs>Programs and Features – Turn Windows features on or off to view this setting)

LAB 6
TROUBLESHOOTING SECURITY

This lab contains the following exercises and activities:

SCENARIO

You have decided to create a highly secure environment for Contoso, using default security levels and additional rules. To implement this policy, you will need to set the default rule to Disallowed and then provide additional rules to allow specific software to run with either the Unrestricted or Basic User security level. You will review events and run the Security Configuration and Analysis Snap-in as part of your security analysis. You will then use the snap-in to complete your security configuration.

After completing this lab, you will be able to:

- Set default security rules.

- Add and modify additional rules.

- Browse, view, and filter events.

- Analyze security policy by using the Security Configuration and Analysis Snap-in.

- Configure security policy by using the Security Configuration and Analysis Snap-in.

Estimated lab time: 60 minutes

Exercise 6.1	Set Default Security Rule via Group Policy
Overview	You will use Group Policy to set the default security rule to Disallowed. By setting the default security rule to Disallowed, you prevent users from running any software. You can then create additional rules that enable users to run specific software.
Completion time	10 minutes

1. With your server started, log on to your Windows Vista client as chrisa. (If the log-on screen displays contoso\chrisa, you can simply key **p@ssw0rd** in the password box and then press Enter.)

2. Create a new GPO as instructed in Exercise 3.2, naming the new GPO **Software Security GPO**. Make sure the new GPO is linked and enabled as instructed in Exercise 3.2.

3. Next, in the Group Policy Management console, right-click the Software Security GPO link under the contoso.com node and then select Edit. The Group Policy Object Editor console is displayed.

4. Expand the User Configuration>Windows Settings>Security Settings nodes and select the Software Restriction Policies node.

5. Right-click the Software Restriction Polices node in the console tree and then click New Software Restriction Policies. This adds a Security Levels node and an Additional Rules node to the Software Restriction Polices node.

6. Select the newly created Security Levels node. Right-click the Disallowed option in the Details pane and then select Properties. The Disallowed Properties dialog box is displayed, as shown in Figure 6-1.

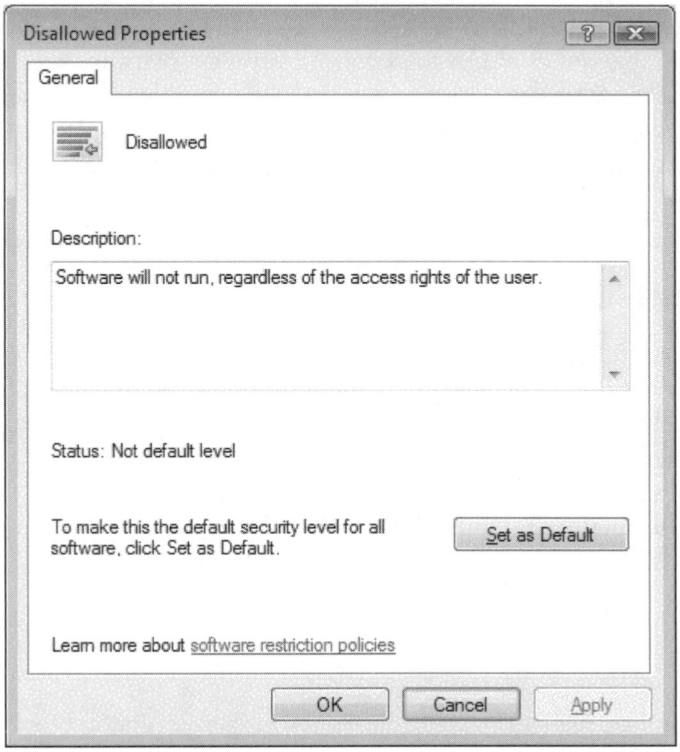

Figure 6-1
The Disallowed Properties dialog box

7. Click Set As default. The Software Restriction Policies dialog box is displayed.

8. Click Yes to close the Software Restriction Policies dialog box.

9. Click OK to close the Disallowed Properties dialog box.

10. Select the Software Restriction Polices node in the console tree, right-click the Enforcement object in the Details pane, and then select Properties. The Enforcement Properties dialog box is displayed.

11. Select the All Users Except Local Administrators option and then click OK.

12. Do not close the consoles.

Question 1	*If you set the default security rule to Disallowed, can anyone run any software?*

Exercise 6.2	Add Specific Rules to Allow Execution
Overview	Now, you will add some specific file type, certificate, hash, network zone, and path rules to enable users to execute software you know to be safe. By adding specific rules to allow users to execute software that you know to be safe, you establish full control over what software will be run throughout the enterprise. Users who want to run additional software will be required to consult with a network administrator to vet the software and add any necessary additional rules to permit the user to run the new software.
Completion time	20 minutes

Add a Rule for File Type

1. Continuing from the previous exercise, in the Group Policy Object Editor console expand the User Configuration>Windows Settings>Security Settings>Software Restriction Policies nodes and select the Software Restriction Policies node.

2. In the Details pane, right-click Designated File Types and then click Properties. The Designated File Types Properties dialog box is displayed.

3. Key **CSO**, Contoso's proprietary executable file extension, in the File Extension text box and then click Add.

4. Click OK to close the Designated File Types Properties dialog box.

Add Additional Rule for Certificate

5. In the Details pane, right-click Additional Rules and then select New Certificate Rule. The New Certificate Rule dialog box is displayed.

6. Click the Browse button. The Open dialog box is displayed.

7. Key **WinSrv03\c$\contoso.cer** in the File Name drop-down list and then click Open. (Your instructor will supply you with the contoso.cer file, which should be installed in the root of the C drive on your server.) The New Certificate Rule dialog box is displayed.

8. In the Security Level drop-down list, select Unrestricted to allow the user to run the software. (Choosing this option enables the user to elevate the software from running with standard user privileges to running with administrator privileges.)

9. Click OK to close the New Certificate Rule dialog box.

Add a Rule for Hash

10. In the Details pane, right-click Additional Rules and then select New Hash Rule. The New Hash Rule dialog box is displayed.

11. Click Browse. The Open dialog box is displayed.

12. Browse to and select C:\Program Files\Internet Explorer\iexplore.exe to identify and restrict it. Note that you must browse to the program's actual location because a hash rule identifies the program based on the contents of the executable file, rather than the name (which can be easily changed). Click Open.

13. In the New Hash Rule dialog box, in the Security level drop-down list, select Basic User to allow the user to run the software, but to prevent the user from elevating the software to run with administrator privileges.

14. In the Description text box, key **Run as basic user only** to explain the purpose of the rule.

15. Click OK to close the New Hash Rule dialog box.

Add a Rule for Network Zone

16. In the Details pane, right-click Additional Rules and then select New Network Zone Rule. The New Network Zone Rule dialog box is displayed.

17. Select Restricted Sites in the Network Zone drop-down list and then select Disallowed in the Security drop-down list.

18. Click OK to close the New Zone Rule dialog box.

Add a Rule for Path

19. In the Details pane, right-click Additional Rules and then select New Path Rule. The New Path Rule dialog box is displayed.

20. Key **%WINDIR%** in the Path text box and make sure the Security Level drop-down list is set to Unrestricted.

21. Click OK to close the New Path Rule dialog box.

22. Select the Additional Rules node in the console tree to view a list of the additional rules you have added, as shown in Figure 6-2.

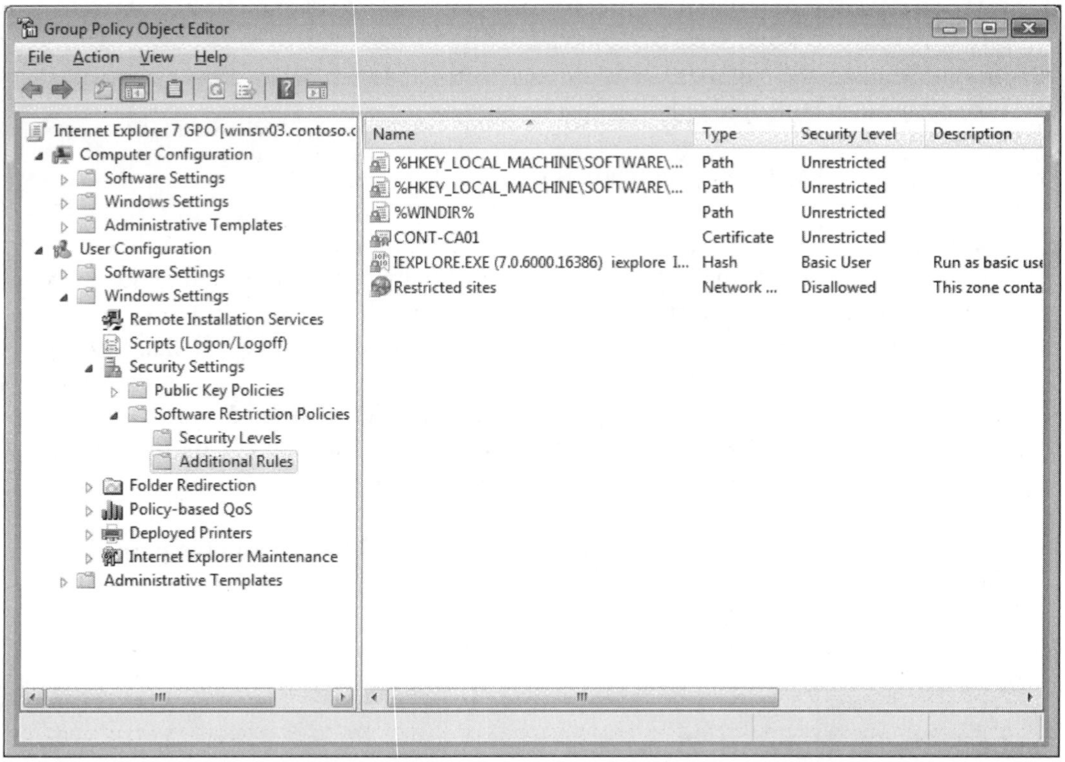

Figure 6-2
The Additional Rules node in the Group Policy Object Editor console

Exercise 6.3 · Modify Hash Rule to Unrestricted Setting	
Overview	You will update the hash rule for Internet Explorer 7 to allow users to run the program without restriction. You have decided that users should be able to run Internet Explorer 7 without restriction, so you need to modify the existing rule that uses a hash value to identify Internet Explorer 7.
Completion time	5 minutes

1. Continuing from the previous exercise, in the Group Policy Object Editor console, make sure the User Configuration>Windows Settings>Security Settings>Software Restriction Policies nodes are expanded and the Additional Rules node is selected.

2. In the Details pane, right-click the IEXPLORE.EXE hash rule and select Properties. The IEXPLORE.EXE Properties dialog box is displayed.

3.   Change the Security Level drop-down list to Unrestricted and then change the description by keying **Run without restrictions**, as shown in Figure 6-3.

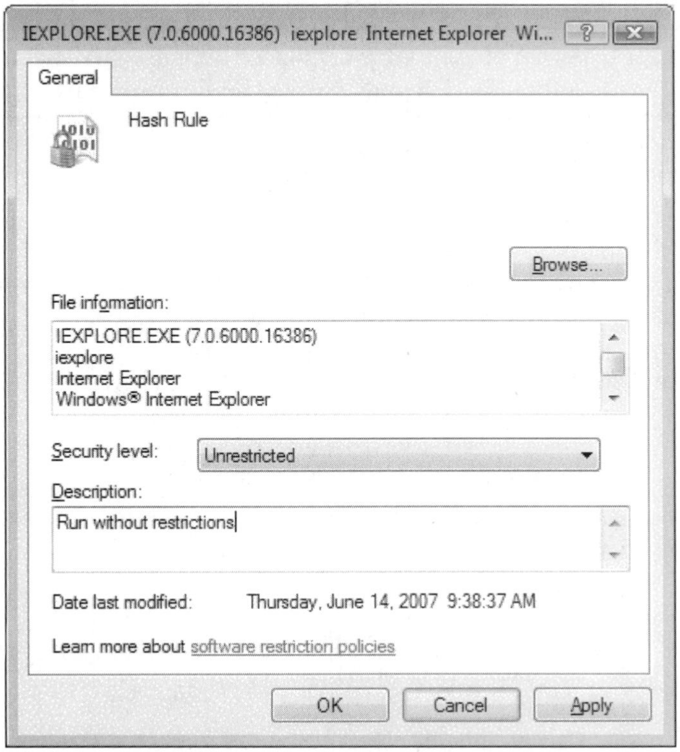

Figure 6-3
The IEXPORE.EXE Properties dialog box

4.   Click OK to close the IEXPORE.EXE Properties dialog box.

5.   Close the Group Policy Object Editor console.

6.   Close the Group Policy Management console.

Question 2	*How can you change the program identified by a hash rule?*

Exercise 6.4	Browse, View, and Filter Events
Overview	You will use Event Viewer to examine a particular event and create a filter for events. You will view details for an individual event. Then you will create a filter to view only Critical and Error events.
Completion time	5 minutes

Browse and View Events

1. Click Start. In the Start Search text box, key **event viewer** and then press Ctrl + Shift + Enter. A User Account Control dialog box is displayed.

2. Provide administrator credentials and then click OK. The Event Viewer console is displayed.

3. In the Details pane, expand the Information Event Type in the Summary Of Administrative Events section. (The events on your system may not match those shown in Figure 6-4.)

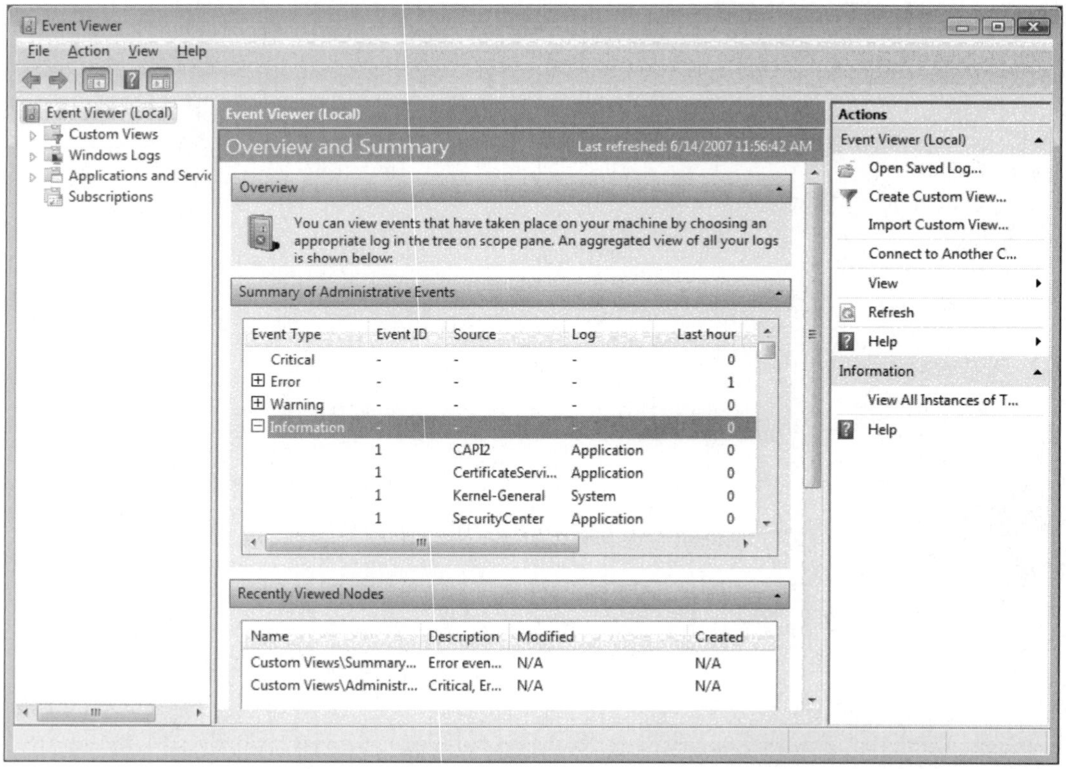

Figure 6-4
The Information event type in the Summary of Administrative Events section of the Event Viewer

4. Scroll through the event types and double-click one that interests you. A list of events is displayed, as shown in Figure 6-5.

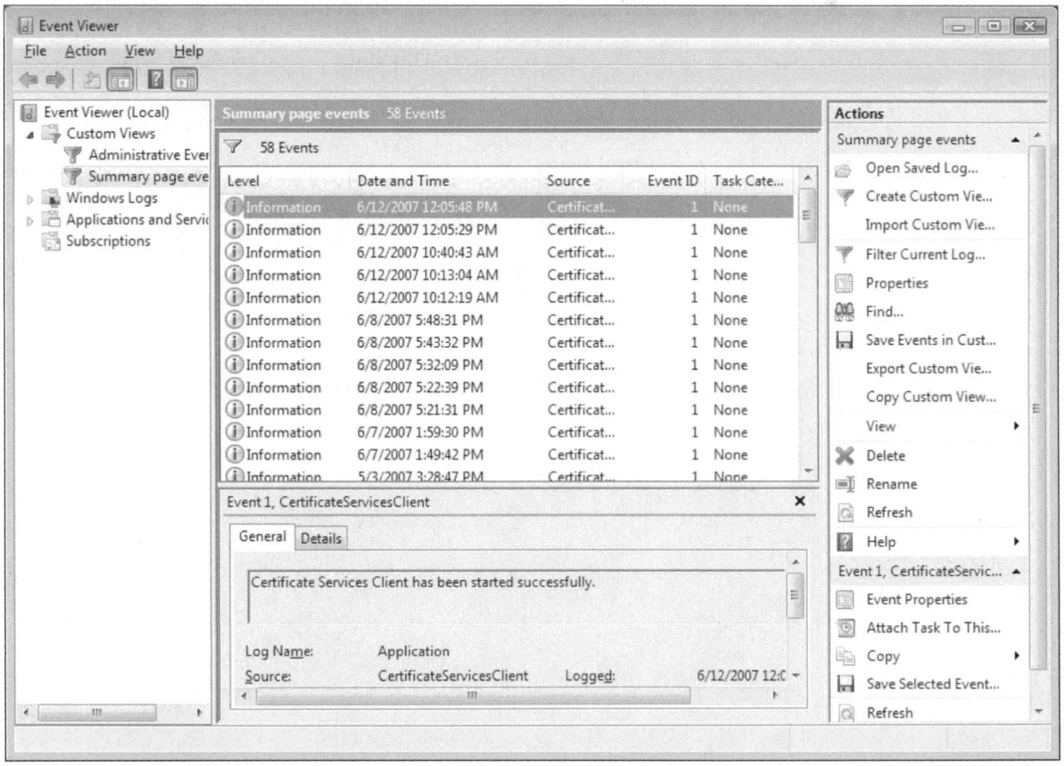

Figure 6-5
A list of events in Event Viewer

5. Again scroll through the events and double-click one. The Event Properties dialog box is displayed, as shown in Figure 6-6. On the General tab and on the Details tab, examine the event you chose.

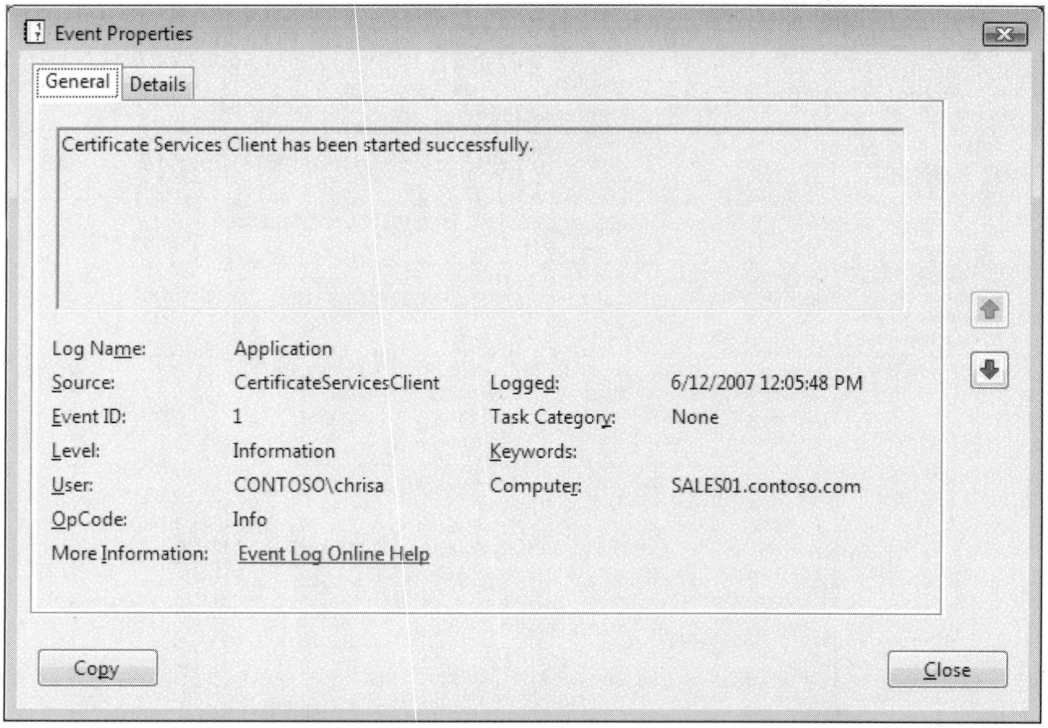

Figure 6-6
The Event Properties dialog box

6. Click Close to close the Event Properties dialog box.

Filter Events

7. In the Event Viewer, expand Windows Logs and then select System.

8. From the Action menu, choose Filter Current Log. The Filter Current Log dialog box is displayed.

9. On the Filter tab, select the Critical and Error checkboxes in the Event Level section and then click OK. This action prevents Warning and Information events from being displayed in the Event Viewer.

10. Close the Event Viewer.

Exercise 6.5	Analyze Settings via Security Configuration and Analysis Snap-In
Overview	You will run the Security Configuration and Analysis Snap-in to compare your security settings against a security template. You want to compare your security policy to a basic policy recommended in the Windows Vista Security Guide. To do so, you will run the Security Configuration and Analysis Snap-in to analyze differences between your security settings and those contained in the VSG EC Desktop.inf security template supplied by the Windows Vista Security Guide.
Completion time	10 minutes

1. Click Start. In the Start Search text box, key **mmc** and then press Ctrl + Shift + Enter. A User Account Control dialog box is displayed.

2. Key your administrator credentials (**netadmin** and **p@ssw0rd**) and click OK. The Microsoft Management console (MMC) is displayed.

3. From the File menu, choose Add/Remove Snap-in. The Add or Remove Snap-ins dialog box is displayed.

4. In the Available Snap-ins list box, select Security Configuration And Analysis and then click Add.

5. Click OK. The Snap-in is added.

6. In the console tree, right-click Security Configuration And Analysis and then click Open Database.

7. Key **Lab06** in the File Name text box and then click Open. This will create a new database named Lab06. The Import Template dialog box is displayed.

 Your Vista client should already have the Windows Vista Security Guide installed. If not, you can download the Windows Vista Security Guide from www.microsoft.com/downloads.

8. In the Import Template dialog box, browse to and select the VSG EC Desktop.inf file in the Users*user*\\Documents\\Windows Vista Security Guide\\GPOAccelerator Tool\\Security Templates folder. Click Open. The template is loaded into the database.

9. Double-click Security Configuration And Analysis in the Details pane to see instructions about how to configure and analyze your computer against the database.

10. Right-click Security Configuration And Analysis in the console tree and then click Analyze Computer Now. The Perform Analysis dialog box appears and displays the default location for the log file. Click OK. After a few seconds, both the console tree and the Details pane are updated with nodes that you can expand and select for information about differences between the Contoso security policies and the security policies in the VSG EC Desktop.inf template, as shown in Figure 6-7.

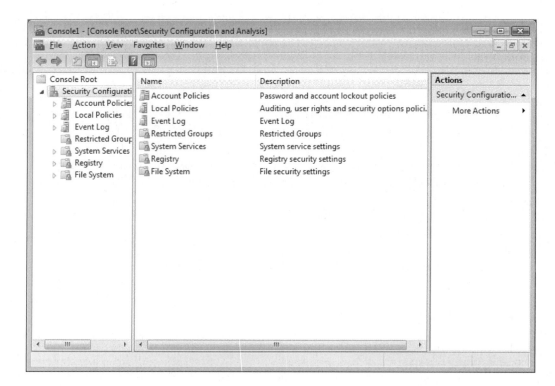

Figure 6-7
Security Configuration and Analysis results

Question 3	*What purpose does the template serve in the Security Configuration and Analysis Snap-in?*

Exercise 6.6	Configure Security Policy via Security Configuration and Analysis Snap-In
Overview	You will update your security policy based on analysis from the Security Configuration and Analysis Snap-in. To implement changes discovered during analysis in the previous exercise, you will use the Security Configuration and Analysis Snap-in to configure your security settings. Before configuring the new policy, you can review the analysis and tell the Security Configuration and Analysis Snap-in which differences to correct and which to leave as is.
Completion time	10 minutes

1. Continuing from the previous exercise, expand the Security Configuration and Analysis>Local Policies node and select the User Rights Assignment node.

2. Notice the red X icon on the second line of the Details pane, labeled Access This Computer From The Network. Double-click this entry. The Access This Computer From The Network Properties dialog box is displayed.

3. Make sure the Define This Policy In The Database checkbox is selected and then click OK.

4. In the Security Configuration and Analysis Snap-in, in the console tree, right-click Security Configuration And Analysis and then click Configure Computer Now. The Configure System dialog box appears and displays the default location for the log file.

5. Click OK. The Configure System Security message box indicates progress until the configuration is complete.

6. Close the Security Configuration And Analysis console. The Microsoft Management Console dialog box is displayed, prompting you to save the console settings. Click No.

LAB REVIEW QUESTIONS

Completion time   10 minutes

1. How can you allow only software that you have approved to run on clients in the enterprise?

2. What are the five levels of events that Windows Vista logs in the event logs? Which of the levels can you select for viewing by using a filter?

3. To add an additional hash rule, why must you browse to the actual program file rather than simply specifying the program name?

LAB CHALLENGE: FORWARD AND COLLECT EVENTS

Completion time   15 minutes

Configure your client to forward events by using the winrm quickconfig command. Specify your client machine's name as the collecting computer. Don't forget to append a dollar sign ($) to the machine name. Next, configure a subscription for forwarded events from that client on the same machine. Examine the events in the Forwarded Events log and save a screenshot of the log in the \\winsrv03\Redirect\Pictures folder as ForwardEventLog.bmp. Your instructor might specify an alternate location, possibly with subfolders for each student.

LAB 7
USING WINDOWS FIREWALL AND WINDOWS DEFENDER

This lab contains the following exercises and activities:

SCENARIO

Contoso's head office has a waiting room for visiting business partners. The waiting room is provisioned with a desktop client for visitors to use. This desktop is not quite as public as a kiosk, but you want to provide slightly higher security, including the ability to manage Windows Firewall remotely and setting more aggressive behavior in Windows Defender.

After completing this lab, you will be able to:

- Turn on and use Windows Firewall.

- Unblock programs in Windows Firewall.

- Use the Windows Firewall with Advanced Security Snap-in to create custom and predefined inbound rules.

- Turn on and use Windows Defender.

- Monitor installed programs by using the Software Explorer tool in Windows Defender.

Estimated lab time: 50 minutes

Exercise 7.1	Turn on Windows Firewall
Overview	You will turn on Windows Firewall at the client that will be available for public use in the visiting partner's waiting room.
Completion time	2 minutes

1. With your server started, log on to your Windows Vista client as chrisa. (If the log-on screen displays contoso\chrisa, you can simply key **p@ssw0rd** in the password box and then press Enter.)

2. Click Start. In the Start Search text box, key **Windows Firewall**. Right-click Windows Firewall in the Programs list and then click Open. The Windows Firewall window is displayed.

3. Click Change Settings. A User Account Control dialog box is displayed.

4. Provide administrator credentials (netadmin and p@ssw0rd) and then click OK. The Windows Firewall Settings dialog box is displayed.

5. On the General tab of the Windows Firewall Settings dialog box, make sure the On (Recommended) option is turned on, as shown in Figure 7-1. This blocks all incoming connections except those unblocked on the Exceptions tab.

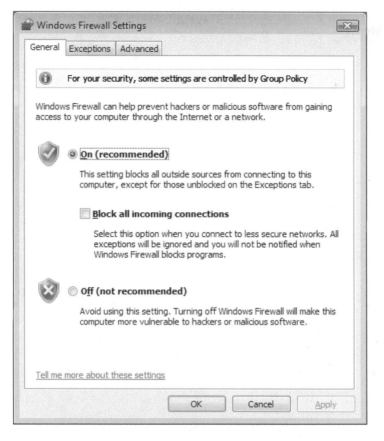

Figure 7-1
Turning on Windows Firewall

6.   Keep the Windows Firewall Settings dialog box open.

Exercise 7.2	Unblock a Program in Windows Firewall
Overview	You will enable the Windows Firewall on your Windows Vista client that is to be managed remotely from an administrator's Windows Vista workstation. To enable the Windows Firewall on your Windows Vista client to be managed remotely from an administrator's Windows Vista workstation, you will establish the appropriate exception in Windows Firewall.
Completion time	5 minutes

1.   In the Windows Firewall Settings dialog box, click the Exceptions tab.

2.   Scroll to find the Windows Firewall Remote Management item in the Program Or Port list box. Select the Windows Firewall Remote Management checkbox, as shown in Figure 7-2, and then click OK.

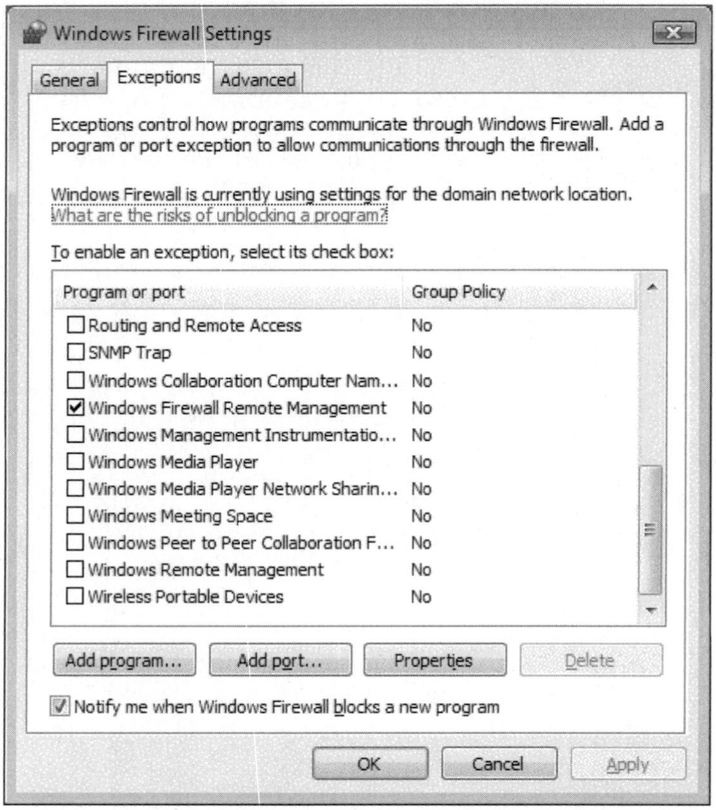

Figure 7-2
Setting an exception for Windows Firewall Remote Management

3. Close the Windows Firewall window.

Exercise 7.3	Open Windows Firewall with Advanced Security Snap-In
Overview	You will open the Windows Firewall with Advanced Security Snap-in in preparation for setting up inbound rules. Because you want to set up inbound rules, you start by opening the Windows Firewall with Advanced Security Snap-in. The snap-in provides more advanced options than the Windows Firewall window you used in the previous two exercises. For example, using the snap-in, you can set Inbound and Outbound rules, set Connection Security Rules, and monitor the Firewall and its rules and associations.
Completion time	5 minutes

1. Click Start. In the Start Search text box, key **Windows Firewall**, right-click Windows Firewall With Advanced Security in the Programs list, and then click Run As Administrator. A User Account Control dialog box is displayed.

2. Provide administrator credentials (**netadmin** and **p@ssw0rd**) and then click OK. The Windows Firewall With Advanced Security Snap-in is displayed, as shown in Figure 7-3.

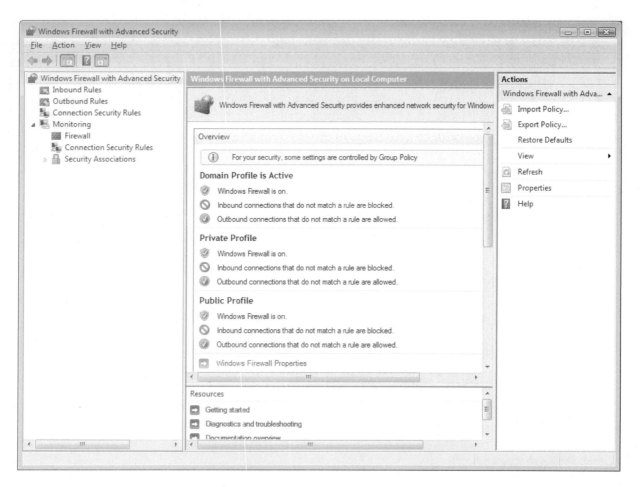

Figure 7-3
The Windows Firewall With Advanced Security Snap-in

3. Keep the Windows Firewall With Advanced Security Snap-in open and proceed to Exercise 7.4.

Question 1	*What are some options that the Windows Firewall With Advanced Security Snap-in offers that are unavailable in the Windows Firewall window?*

Exercise 7.4	Create a Custom Inbound Rule
Overview	You will configure an inbound rule to require secure connections. Because you can't be certain how users will use the client in the waiting room, you want to require that inbound connections be authenticated and integrity-protected through Internet Protocol Security (IPsec).
Completion time	10 minutes

1. With the Windows Firewall With Advanced Security Snap-in still open, select Inbound Rules in the console tree.

2. From the Action menu, click New Rule. The New Inbound Rule Wizard is displayed.

3. Select Custom and then click Next. The *Program* page is displayed.

4. Select All Programs and click Next. The *Protocol And Ports* page is displayed.

5. In the Protocol Type drop-down list, select Any and click Next. The *Scope* page is displayed.

6. On the *Scope* page, under Which Local IP Address Does This Rule Match, select Any IP Address. Under Which Remote IP Address Does This Rule Match, select Any IP Address. Click Next. The *Action* page is displayed.

7. On the *Action* page, select Allow The Connection If It Is Secure. This allows the connection only if it is secured using IPsec. Leave the Require The Connections To Be Encrypted and Override Block Rules checkboxes unchecked, as shown in Figure 7-4.

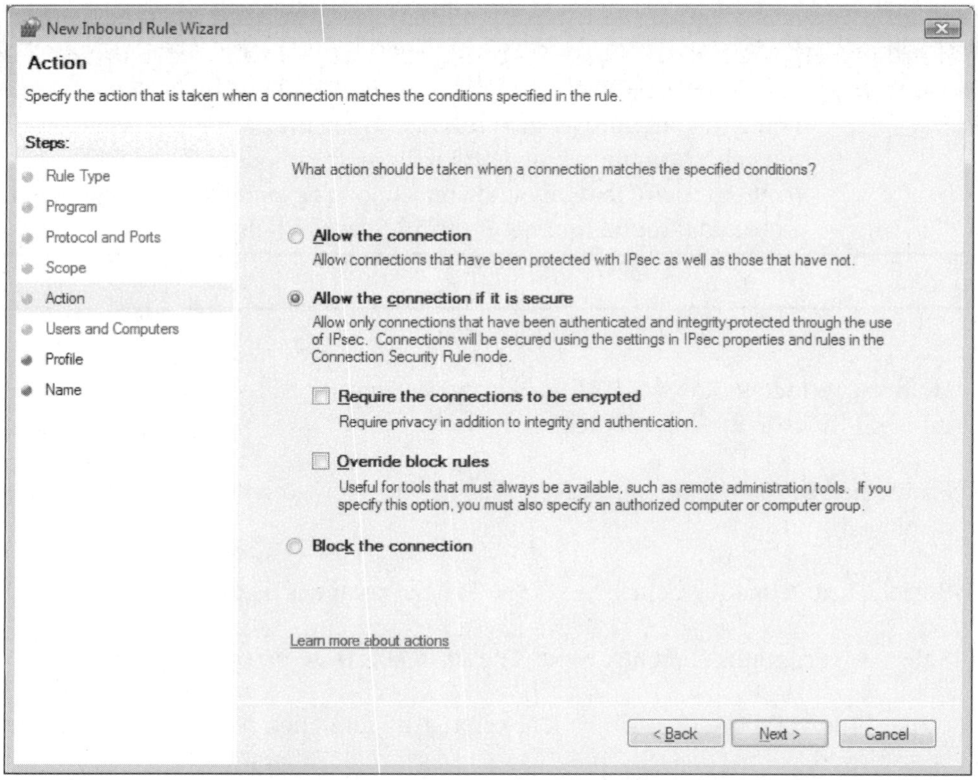

Figure 7-4
The *Action* page of the New Inbound Rule Wizard

8. Click Next on the *Action* page. The *Users And Computers* page is displayed.

9. Click Next. The *Profile* page is displayed. Check the Domain, Private, and Public checkboxes and then click Next. The *Name* page is displayed.

10. In the Name text box, key **Waiting Room Rule**. In the Description text box, key **Rule for public client in waiting room**. Click Finish. The rule is added to the Inbound Rules list.

Exercise 7.5	Create a Predefined Inbound Rule
Overview	You will ensure that Windows Firewall Remote Management is not blocked by security settings. This procedure enables you to verify that security settings will not interfere with using Windows Firewall Remote Management. The predefined rules are designed to provide the necessary security settings to enable a particular set of Windows functionality. Because a predefined rule can include a group of rules governing a variety of settings, this significantly reduces the time and potential for errors in implementing a security policy.
Completion time	10 minutes

1. With the Windows Firewall With Advanced Security Snap-in open, select Inbound Rules in the console tree. From the Action menu, click New Rule. The New Inbound Rule Wizard is displayed.

2. Select Predefined. In the corresponding drop-down list, select Windows Firewall Remote Management, as shown in Figure 7-5.

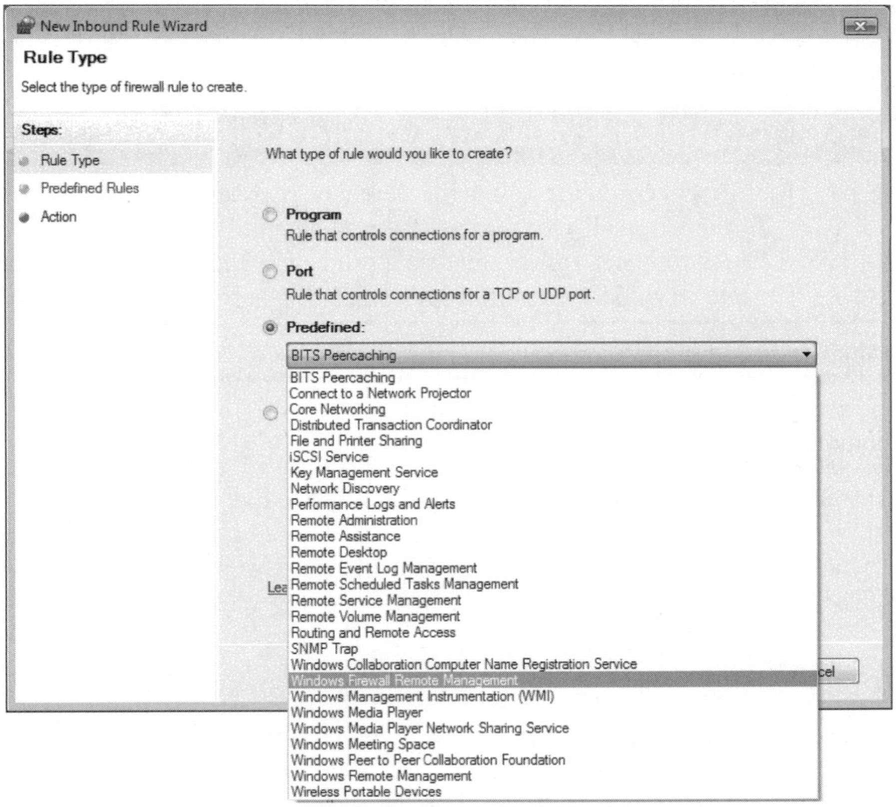

Figure 7-5
The *Rule Type* page of the New Inbound Rule Wizard

3. Click Next. The *Predefined Rules* page is displayed.

4. In the Rules list box, select all the rules and click Next. The *Action* page is displayed.

	If a rule is listed as already existing in the Rule Exists column on the Predefined Rules page of the New Inbound Rule Wizard, selecting it will ensure that any previous modifications to the rule are overwritten, effectively resetting the rule to its initial definition.

5. Select Allow The Connection If It Is Secure and click Next. The *Users And Computers* page is displayed.

6. On the *Users And Computers* page, click Finish. The group of rules is added to the Inbound Rules list.

7. Close the Windows Firewall With Advanced Security Snap-In.

Question 2	*What is the advantage of using a predefined rule?*

Exercise 7.6	Configure Windows Defender Options
Overview	You will configure Windows Defender. You have decided to use Windows Defender on all your clients. Turning on and configuring Windows Defender gives a client real-time protection and idle-time scanning protection against viruses, spyware, and other malicious software.
Completion time	15 minutes

1. Click Start. In the Start Search text box, key **Windows Defender** and then press Ctrl + Shift + Enter. A User Account Control message box is displayed.

2. Provide administrator credentials (netadmin and p@ssw0rd) and then click OK. Windows Defender opens.

3. Click Tools. The *Tools And Settings* page is displayed.

4. In the Settings section, click Options. The *Options* page is displayed.

5. In the Automatic scanning section, select the Automatically Scan My Computer (Recommended) checkbox. In the Frequency drop-down list, select Sunday to scan on that day only (once per week). In the Approximate time drop-down list, select 2:00 AM. In the Type drop-down list, select (Full System Scan). Verify

that the Check for updated definitions before scanning checkbox and the Apply default actions to items detected during a scan checkbox are selected, as shown in Figure 7-6.

> **NOTE**
>
> *A quick scan will check only the places on the client that are most likely to be infected by malicious software. A full system scan will check all files as well as currently running programs.*

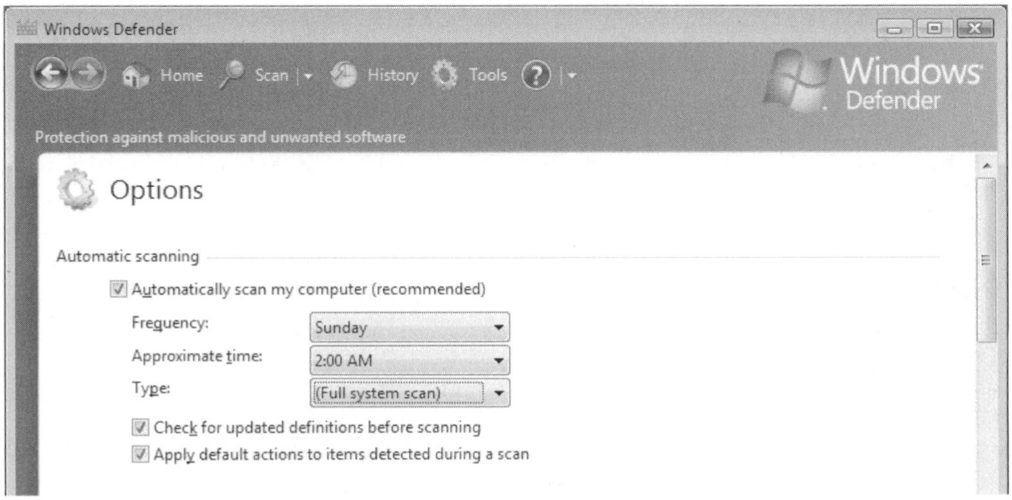

Figure 7-6
The Automatic Scanning section of the *Windows Defender Options* page

6. In the Default Actions section, select Remove in the High Alert Items drop-down list to remove the detected item automatically, as shown in Figure 7-7.

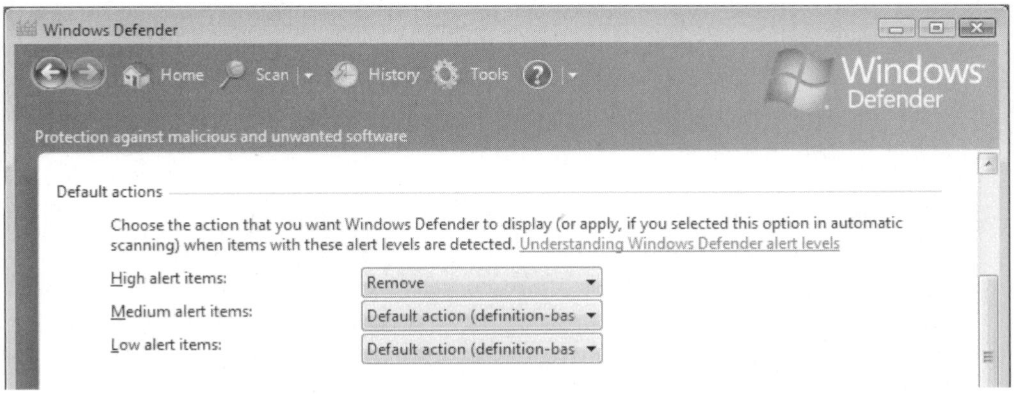

Figure 7-7
The Default Actions section of the *Windows Defender Options* page

7. Scroll to the Real-time Protection Options section and select the Use Real-time Protection (Recommended) checkbox.

8. Under the Choose If Windows Defender should notify you about section, select the Software that has not yet been classified for risks checkbox and the Changes made to your computer by software that is permitted to run checkbox.

9. Under the Choose When The Windows Defender Icon appears in the notification area section, select Always, as shown in Figure 7-8.

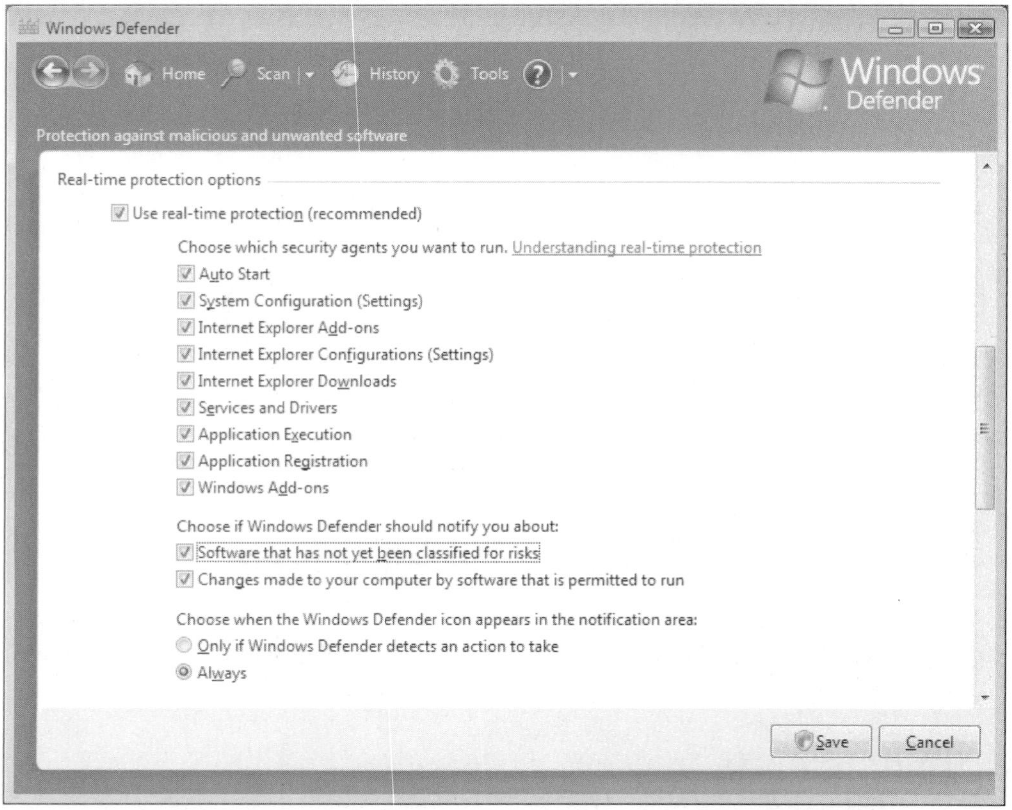

Figure 7-8
The Real-time Protection Options section of the *Windows Defender Options* page

10. On the *Options* page, scroll to the Advanced Options section. Uncheck the Scan The Contents Of The Archived Files And Folders For Potential Threats checkbox and the Create A Restore Point Before Applying Actions To Detected Items checkbox. Verify that the Use heuristics to detect potentially harmful or unwanted behavior by software that hasn't been analyzed for risks checkbox is selected.

11. On the *Options* page, scroll to the Administrator Options section. Verify that the Use Windows Defender checkbox is selected, but turn off the Allow everyone to use Windows Defender checkbox, as shown in Figure 7-9.

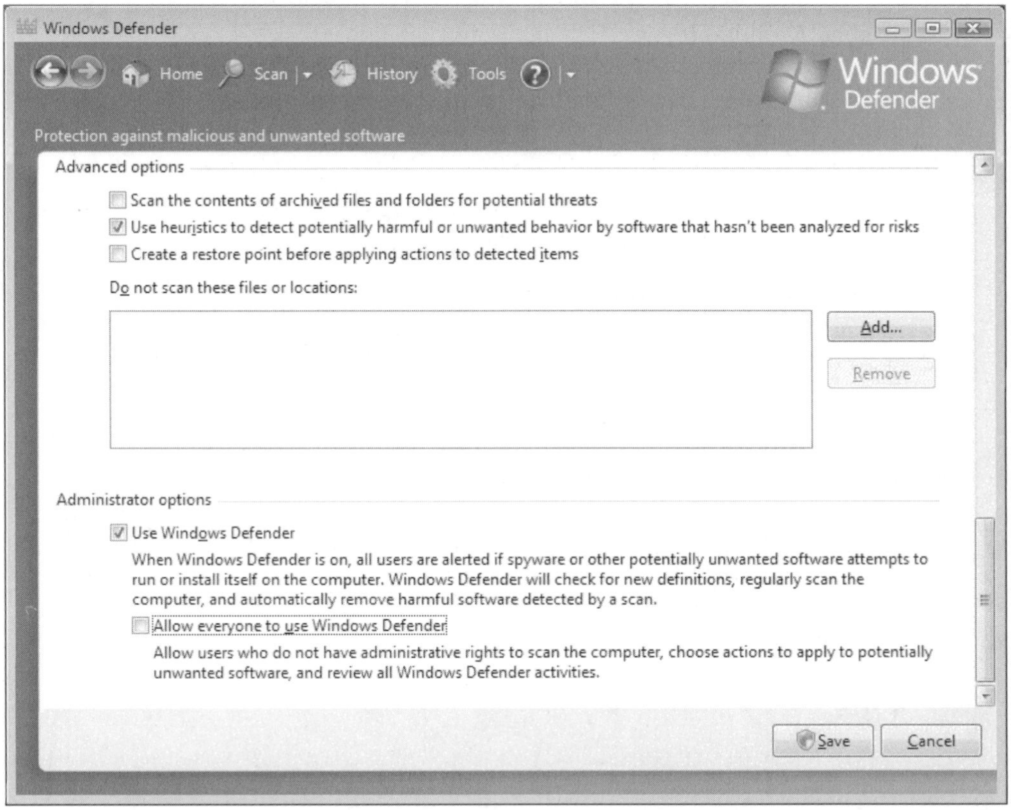

Figure 7-9
The Advanced Options and Administrator Options sections at the bottom of the *Windows Defender Options* page

12. In the Windows Defender window, click Save. A User Account Control dialog box is displayed.

13. Provide administrator credentials (netadmin and p@ssw0rd) and then click OK.

14. Keep Windows Defender open and proceed to the next exercise.

Question 3	*What are the two main ways in which Windows Defender can protect a client?*

Exercise 7.7	Use Software Explorer to Review Startup Programs
Overview	You will use Software Explorer to review the programs that run automatically when the client starts up. Verify that only programs you know about and expect are scheduled to run at startup on your waiting room desktop.
Completion time	3 minutes

1. Open Windows Defender if necessary and display the *Tools And Settings* page, as shown in Figure 7-10. Refer to steps 1 through 3 in Exercise 7.7 if necessary.

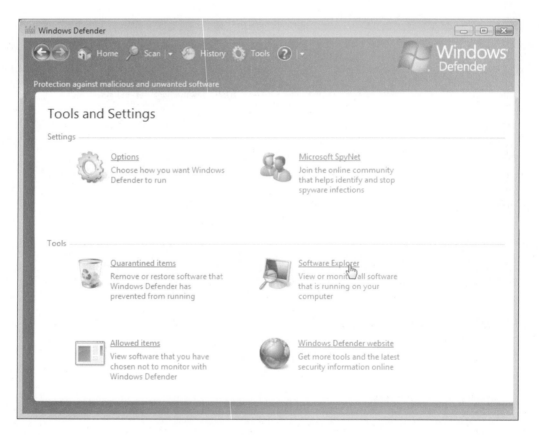

Figure 7-10
The Windows Defender *Tools And Settings* page

2. In the Tools section of the *Tools And Settings* page, click Software Explorer. The *Software Explorer* page is displayed.

3. Click Show For All Users. A User Account Control dialog box is displayed. Provide administrator credentials (netadmin and p@ssw0rd) and then click OK.

4. In the Category drop-down list, select Startup Programs. Review the programs listed in the Name column, as shown in Figure 7-11. If a program is listed that you don't want to run at startup on this client, select the program in the Name column and click the Remove button.

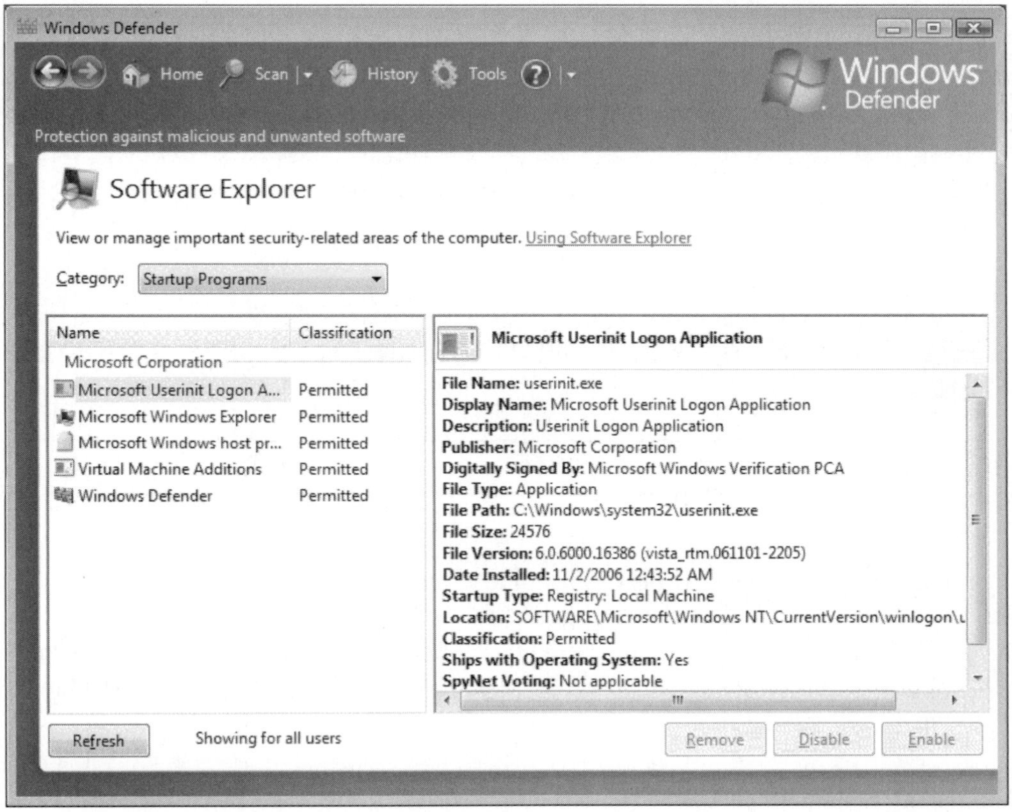

Figure 7-11
Software Explorer, showing startup programs for all users

LAB REVIEW QUESTIONS

Completion time	10 minutes

1. What utility on Windows Vista provides protection against an outside program using the network to attack a client? What utility on Windows Vista provides protection against a malicious program running internally on a client?

2. What is the advantage to using a predefined rule instead of a custom rule in Windows Firewall with Advanced Security? What are the limitations?

3. How does a Windows Defender quick scan differ from a full scan?

LAB CHALLENGE: SCAN YOUR SYSTEM MANUALLY WITH WINDOWS DEFENDER

Completion time	20 minutes

Open Windows Defender and perform a quick scan of the system. Note the elapsed time of the scan. Save a screenshot of the results report in the \\winsrv03\Redirect\Pictures folder as QuickScan.bmp. Run a full system scan and again note the elapsed time. How much longer does a full system scan take than a quick scan?

LAB 8
TROUBLESHOOTING ACCESS, AUTHENTICATION, AND USER ACCOUNT CONTROL ISSUES

THIS LAB CONTAINS THE FOLLOWING EXERCISES AND ACTIVITIES:

SCENARIO

At Contoso, you have decided to increase security by requiring explicit consent for credential elevation. Several of your users share a client that has sensitive data. You must allow them to access the shared file but protect it from other users. You have also decided to use Group Policy to encrypt the contents of everyone's Document folder, and to change your Certification Authority to require an administrator's approval when a certificate is requested.

After completing this lab, you will be able to:

- Use Group Policy to configure User Account Control settings.

- Use the EFS Wizard.

- Export and import certificates.

- Share encrypted files among several users.

- Use Group Policy to configure and implement EFS settings.

- Change the way in which a Certification Authority processes certificate requests.

- Renew certificates on a client.

- Approve certificates by using Certification Authority.

Estimated lab time: 55 minutes

Exercise 8.1	Configure UAC Group Policy Settings
Overview	You will use Group Policy to configure User Account Control (UAC) settings. You want to implement a policy that will require administrators to actively consent to elevating their privileges when starting an operation that requires administrator credentials. Because you know that certain users will install programs in addition to those rolled out by the enterprise, you also want to let the system detect installation applications and prompt for elevation. Otherwise, those installation applications will fail. This way, the user will be notified before starting the installation if elevated credentials are required.
Completion time	10 minutes

1. With your server started, log on to your Windows Vista client as chrisa. (If the log-on screen displays contoso\chrisa, you can simply key **p@ssw0rd** in the Password box and then press Enter.)

2. Create a new GPO as instructed in Exercise 3.2, giving the new GPO the name **UAC GPO**. Make sure the new GPO is linked and enabled as instructed in Exercise 3.2.

3. In the Group Policy Management console, right-click the UAC GPO link under the contoso.com node and then select Edit. The Group Policy Object Editor console is displayed.

4. In the console tree, expand Computer Configuration>Windows Settings>Security Settings>Local Policies and then select Security Options.

5. In the Details pane, scroll to the bottom to find the User Account Control policies. Double-click the User Account Control: Admin Approval Mode For The Built-in Administrator Account item. The User Account Control: Admin Approval Mode For The Built-in Administrator Account dialog box is displayed.

6. Turn on the Define This Policy Setting checkbox, select the Enabled option, and then click OK.

Consider setting the User Account Control: Behavior Of The Elevation Prompt For Standard Users policy to Automatically Deny Elevation Requests. However, this can interfere with a policy intended to allow administrators to log on as standard users and elevate their credentials only when necessary.

7. Double-click the User Account Control: Detect application Installations And Prompt For Elevation item. The User Account Control: Detect Application Installations And Prompt For Elevation dialog box is displayed.

8. Turn on the Define This Policy Setting checkbox, select the Enabled option, and then click OK.

9. Close the Group Policy Object Editor console.

10. Close the Group Policy Management console.

Exercise 8.2	Use the Encrypting File System Wizard to Update Encrypted Files
Overview	You will use the Encrypting File System (EFS) Wizard to update the encryption for a folder and its contents. A user, John Tippett, has sensitive data in his Desktop folder. He has already encrypted the data by using the Advanced button in the File Properties dialog box, but you have advised him that he should update the encryption by using a certificate from the enterprise's Certificate Authority. To update the encrypted files, you will step him through the EFS Wizard. Completing this wizard will enhance the security of the encryption and allow him to share the encrypted file with others whom he trusts when they use his client.
Completion time	5 minutes

Your server should be set up as a Certification Authority. This exercise also assumes your Vista client has an encrypted folder named Sales data containing a file named sales.txt in the root of the C drive and that the files were encrypted by the user johnt using the Advanced button on the file Properties dialog box.

NOTE

The scenario presented in Exercises 8.2 thorugh 8.5 is common when a laptop with sensitive data is shared by multiple people, some of whom need to share access to the sensitive data.

NOTE

1.   Still logged on to your Windows Vista client as chrisa, click Start and then click the right arrow to the right of the Search box. Click Switch User. A startup screen is displayed.

2.   Press Ctrl + Alt + Delete. To log on as John Tippett, key **johnt** in the User Name text box, key **p@ssw0rd** in the Password text box, and then press Enter.

3.   Click Start and then click Control Panel. The Control Panel window is displayed.

4.   Click User Accounts. The User Accounts window is displayed.

5.   Click User Accounts again. A second User Accounts window is displayed, as shown in Figure 8-1.

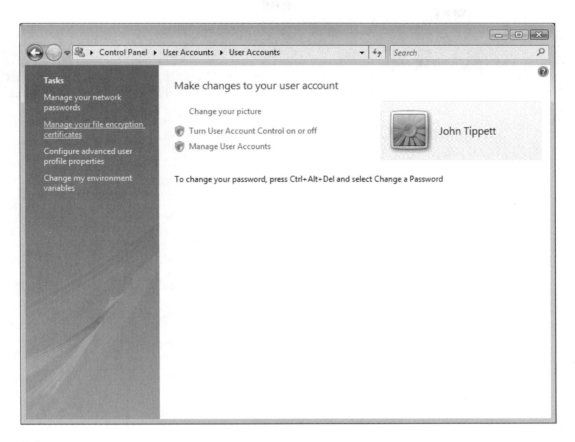

Figure 8-1
The second User Accounts window

6.   In the left navigation bar, click Manage Your File Encryption Certificates. The Encrypting File System Wizard is displayed.

7.   Click Next. The *Select Or Create A File Encryption Certificate* page is displayed.

8.   Select Create A New Certificate and then click Next. The next page of the wizard prompts you for the type of certificate you want to create, as shown in Figure 8-2.

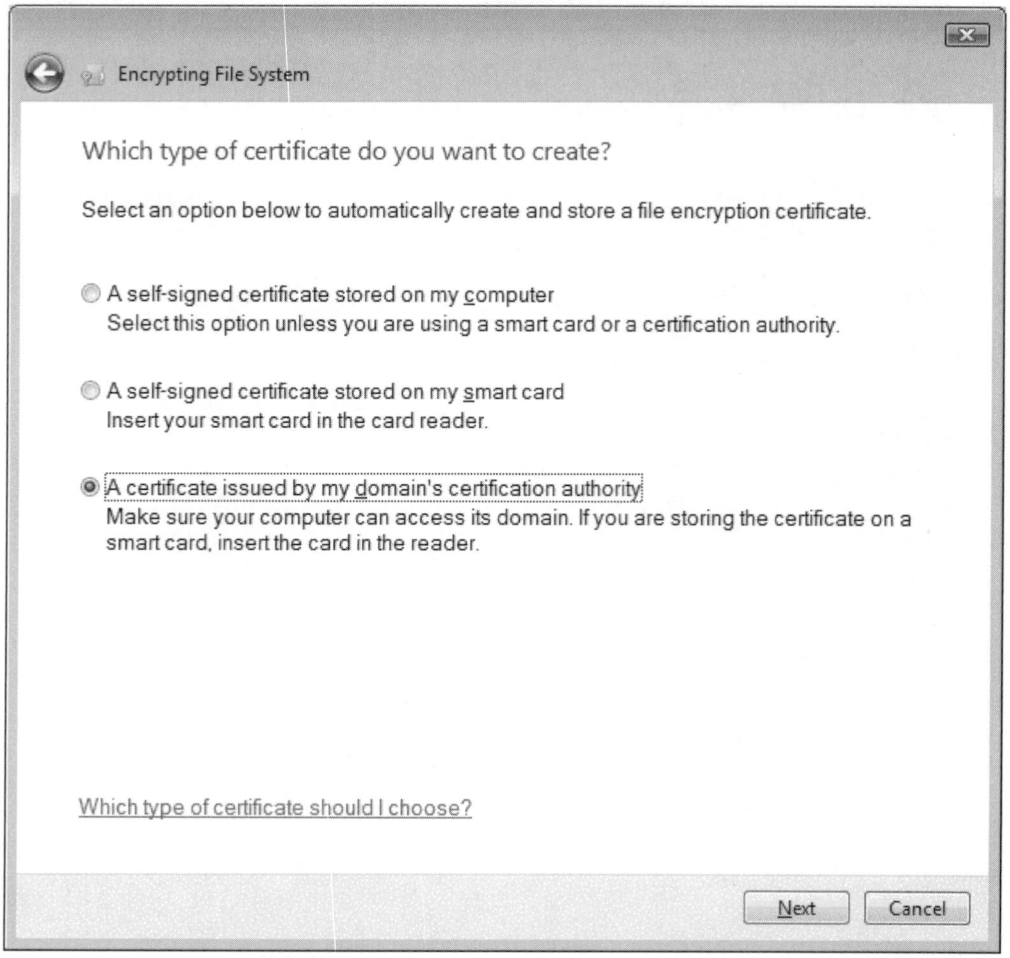

Encrypting File System

Which type of certificate do you want to create?

Select an option below to automatically create and store a file encryption certificate.

○ A self-signed certificate stored on my computer
Select this option unless you are using a smart card or a certification authority.

○ A self-signed certificate stored on my smart card
Insert your smart card in the card reader.

◉ A certificate issued by my domain's certification authority
Make sure your computer can access its domain. If you are storing the certificate on a smart card, insert the card in the reader.

Which type of certificate should I choose?

Next   Cancel

Figure 8-2
The EFS Wizard prompts you for the type of certificate to create

9. Select A Certificate Issued By My Domain's Certification Authority and click Next. The *Back Up The Certificate And Key* page of the EFS Wizard is displayed.

10. Click the Browse button and key **TippettCertificateBackup** in the File Name text box and then click Save. Key **p@ssw0rd** in the Password and Confirm Password text boxes.

Normally, you would back up the certificate and key to removable media and choose a password specific to this certificate, rather than using the same password that you use for logging on.

11. Click Next. The *Update Your Previously Encrypted Files* page of the EFS Wizard is displayed, as shown in Figure 8-3.

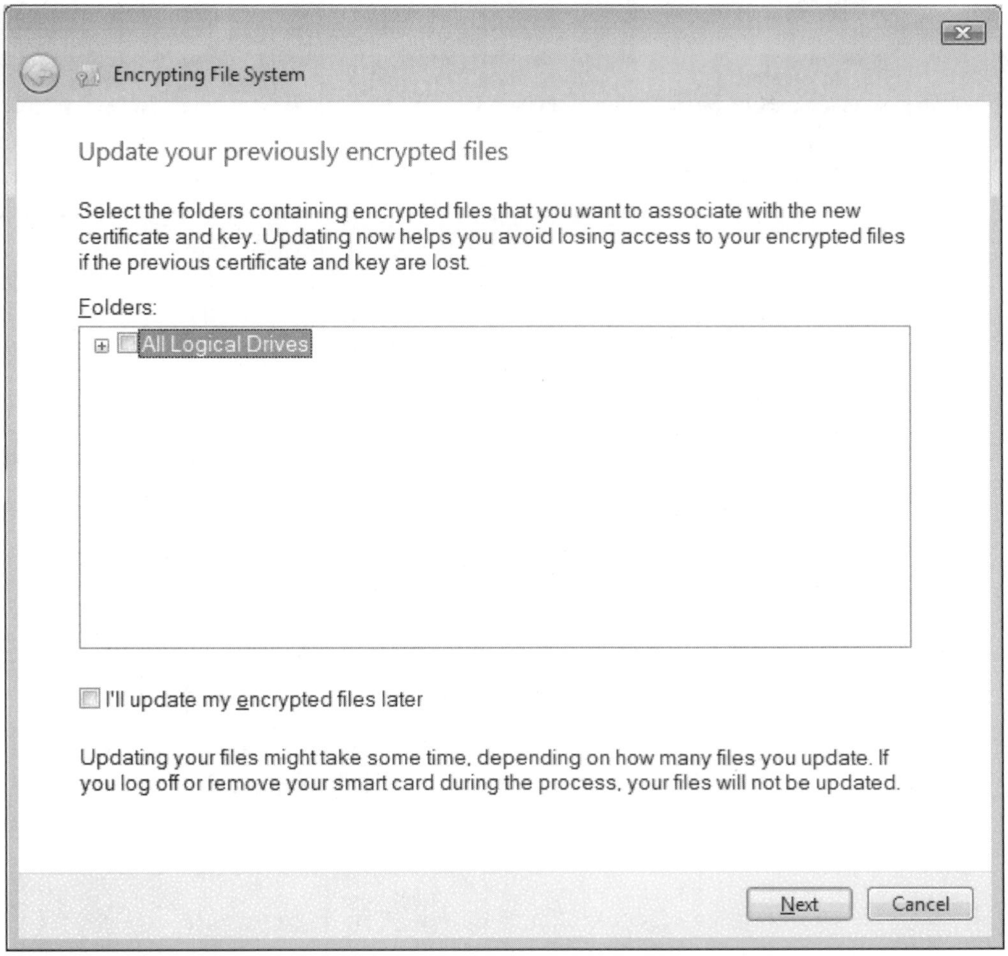

Figure 8-3
The Update Your Previously Encrypted Files page of the EFS Wizard

12. In the Folders tree, expand All Logical Drives>C:\>folders and check in the Sales Data checkbox. (The EFS Wizard will not affect files that have not already been encrypted.) Click Next. The *Your Encrypted Files Have Been Updated* page of the EFS Wizard is displayed.

13. Click Close to close the wizard.

Question 1	*Which files are updated by the EFS Wizard?*

Exercise 8.3	Export an EFS Certificate
Overview	You will export an EFS certificate for use by others. Because John Tippett wants the ability to share the secure data on his client with another member of his subcommittee who may log on to his client, you will have the other person export an EFS certificate used to encrypt her files. John Tippett can then import the other user's EFS certificate and add it to the encrypted file so that the other user can transparently use the encrypted file. The file is protected from all users other than John Tippett and any users whom he explicitly trusts by adding their certificate.
Completion time	10 minutes

1. Still logged on as John Tippett, click Start and then click the right arrow to the right of the Search box. Click Switch User. A startup window is displayed.

2. Press Ctrl + Alt + Delete. To log on as Sheela Word, key **sheelaw** in the User Name textbox, key **p@ssw0rd** in the Password text box, and then press Enter.

3. To check whether you can access the encrypted sales.txt file, try to open it by double-clicking the file in Windows Explorer, or you can key **c:\Sales data\sales.txt** in the Start Search box. An Access is Denied message box is displayed. Click OK and close Notepad if necessary.

4. To create a certificate, repeat steps 3 through 9 in Exercise 8.2.

5. On the *Back Up The Certificate And Key* page of the EFS Wizard, click the Browse button and key **WordCertificateBackup** in the File Name text box. Then click Save. Key **p@ssw0rd** in the Password and Confirm Password text boxes.

6. Click Next. The *Update Your Previously Encrypted Files* page of the EFS Wizard is displayed.

7. Click Next without selecting any folders to update. Then close the wizard.

8. In the Start Search text box, key **certmgr.msc** and then press Enter. The Microsoft Management Console (MMC) is displayed with the Certificate Manager snap-in loaded.

9. In the console tree, expand Personal and then select Certificates.

10. In the Details pane, right-click the certificate issued to Sheela Word, point to All Tasks, and then click Export. The Certificate Export Wizard is displayed.

11. In the Certificate Export Wizard, click Next. The *Export Private Key* page is displayed.

12. Select No, Do Not Export The Private Key. Click Next. The *Export File Format* page is displayed.

13. Click Next. The *File to Export* page is displayed.

> **NOTE** *Normally, you would choose a password specific to this certificate, rather than using the same password that you use for logging on.*

14. Click Browse. The Save As dialog box is displayed.

15. Click the Browse Folders button. Click the More button in the Favorite Links area and select Public. Double-click the Public Documents folder.

> **NOTE** *Normally, you would instruct Sheela Word to export her certificate to a private location, such as her Documents folder, and then transfer the file to John Tippett via email.*
>
> *Alternatively, Sheela Word could export the certificate to removable media, such as a flash drive, and then physically transfer the media to John Tippett. After John Tippett has imported the certificate and returned the removable media, Sheela Word should delete the certificate from the media.*

16. Key **SheelaWordCertificate** in the File Name text box and click Save. Click Next on the *File To Export* page. The *Completing The Certificate Export Wizard* page is displayed.

17. Click Finish. The Certificate Export Wizard message box is displayed.

18. Click OK. Close the Certificate Manager snap-in.

Exercise 8.4	Import a Certificate from a Trusted Person
Overview	You will import a certificate. John Tippett can now import Sheela Word's certificate, designating her as a trusted person.
Completion time	5 minutes

1. Continuing from Exercise 8.3, click Start and then click the right arrow to the right of the Search box. Click Switch User. A startup window is displayed.

2. Press Ctrl + Alt + Delete. To reconnect to John Tippett's log-on session, key **johnt** in the User Name textbox, key **p@ssw0rd** in the Password text box, and then press Enter.

3. Click Start. In the Start Search text box, key **certmgr.msc** and then press Enter. The Microsoft Management Console (MMC) is displayed with the Certificate Manager snap-in loaded.

4. In the Certificate Manager snap-in, in the console tree, right-click Trusted People, point to All Tasks, and then select Import. The Certificate Import Wizard is displayed.

5. Click Next. The *File To Import* page is displayed.

6. Click Browse. The Open dialog box is displayed.

7. In the Favorite Links area, click Public and then double-click Public Documents in the Details pane.

8. Double-click the SheelaWordCertificate file. On the *File To Import* page, click Next. The *Certificate Store* page is displayed.

9. Verify that the Place All Certificates In The Following Store option is selected and Trusted People is listed in the Certificate Store box. Click Next. The *Completing the Certificate Import Wizard* page is displayed.

10. Click Finish. The Certificate Import Wizard message box is displayed.

11. Click OK. Close the Certificate Manager snap-in.

Question 2	*Does importing a person's certificate allow them to read files that you have encrypted?*

Exercise 8.5	Add a Trusted Person's Certificate to Share an Encrypted File
Overview	You will add a certificate to an encrypted file. Because Sheela Word has been added as a trusted person, John Tippett can add her certificate to any encrypted file to which he wants to give her access. This way, a user can share selected files with various users without exposing all encrypted files. To test your work, Sheela Word will try to access the encrypted file.
Completion time	5 minutes

1. Click Start>All Programs>Accessories>Windows Explorer.

2. In Windows Explorer, browse to C:\Sales data. Right-click the sales.txt file and click Properties. The Sales Properties dialog box is displayed.

3. Click Advanced. The Advanced Attributes dialog box is displayed.

4. Click Details. The User Access to C:\Sales data\sales.txt dialog box is displayed, as shown in Figure 8-4.

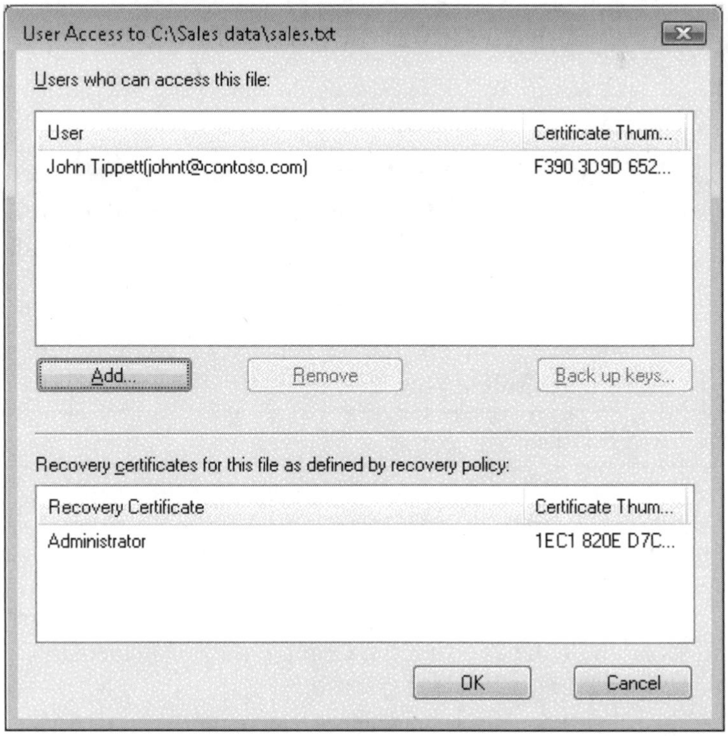

Figure 8-4
The User Access to C:\Sales data\sales.txt dialog box

5. Click Add. The Encrypting File System dialog box is displayed.

6. From the list of certificates, select the certificate issued to Sheela Word and then click OK.

7. Click OK to close the User Access to C:\Sales data\sales.txt dialog box.

8. Click OK to close the Advanced Attributes dialog box.

9. Click OK to close the Sales Properties dialog box.

10. Close Windows Explorer and log off as John Tippett. A startup window is displayed.

11. To verify that Sheela Word can now access the encrypted sales.txt file, press Ctrl + Alt + Delete. To reconnect to Sheela Word's log-on session, key **sheelaw** in the User Name text box, key **p@ssw0rd** in the Password text box, and then press Enter. Try to open the encrypted file by double-clicking the file in Windows Explorer, or you can key **c:\Sales data\sales.txt** in the Start Search box. Notepad should start, displaying the contents of the encrypted file as normal text. Close Notepad.

12. Stay logged on as Sheela Word to complete the remaining exercises.

Question 3	*What is the advantage of adding certificates on a per-file basis, rather than giving a user access to all files you encrypt?*

Exercise 8.6	Configure EFS Group Policy Settings
Overview	You will use EFS Group Policy settings to encrypt all users' Documents folders. To ensure that the files your users use on a daily basis cannot be compromised, you have decided that all users should encrypt their Documents folders. Rather than having each user do so, you will use Group Policy to roll out this new mandate.
Completion time	5 minutes

1. Still logged on to your Windows Vista client as sheelaw, click Start.

2. In the Start Search text box, key **gpmc.msc** and then press Ctrl + Shift + Enter to use administrator credentials to start the Group Policy Management console (GPMC). A User Account Control dialog box is displayed.

3. Key your administrator name and password (netadmin and p@ssw0rd). Click OK. The Group Policy Management console is displayed.

4. In the Group Policy Management console tree, expand Forest: contoso.com>Domains>contoso.com. Right-click the UAC GPO policy and click Edit. The Group Policy Object Editor is displayed.

NOTE	*To implement different encryption policies depending on user groups, create appropriate Organization Units and link them to different GPOs in the Group Policy Management console.*

5. In the Group Policy Object Editor, in the console tree, expand Computer Configuration>Windows Settings>Security Settings>Public Key Policies.

6. Right-click Encrypting File System and then click Properties. The Encrypting File System Properties dialog box is displayed.

7. Under File Encryption Using Encrypting File System (EFS), select Allow. Turn on the Encrypt The Contents Of The User's Documents Folder option, the Enable Pagefile Encryption option, and the Display Key Backup Notifications When User Key Is Created Or Changed option, as shown in Figure 8-5. Click OK.

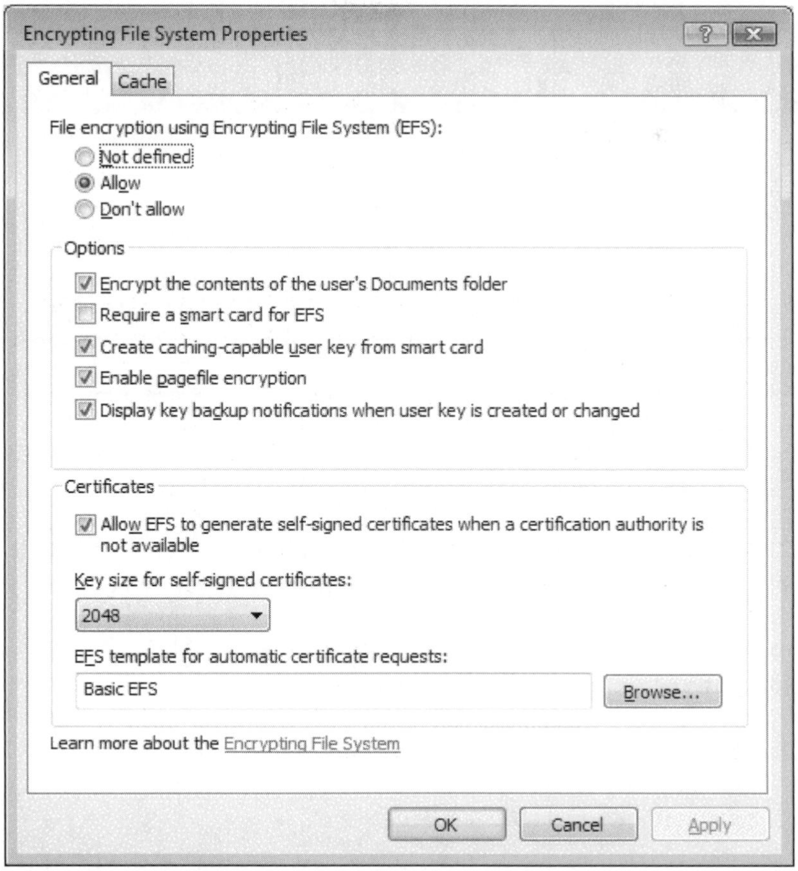

Figure 8-5
The Encrypting File System Properties dialog box.

8.   Click OK to close the Encrypting File System Properties dialog box.

9.   Close the Group Policy Object Editor console.

10.   Close the Group Policy Management console.

Exercise 8.7	Set Certificate Authority to Review Requests
Overview	You will set your Certificate Authority so that an administrator must review and approve all certificate requests. By setting your Certificate Authority so that an administrator must approve all certificate requests, you can ensure that users are appropriately using encryption on their clients. The manual intervention gives you a chance to educate users as needed when they work with EFS.
Completion time	5 minutes

1. Log on to Windows Server 2003 with your administrator account (netadmin and p@ssw0rd).

2. Click Start>Administrative Tools>Certification Authority. The Certification Authority console is displayed. Select the CONT-CA01 certification authority in the console tree.

3. From the Action menu, select Properties. The CONT-CA01 Properties dialog box is displayed.

4. Select the Policy Module tab, as shown in Figure 8-6.

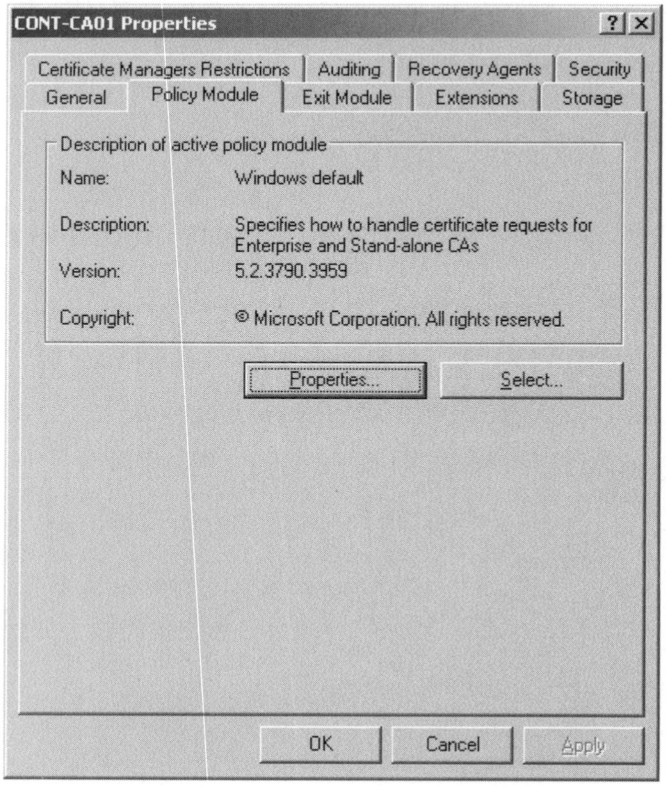

Figure 8-6
The Policy Module tab of the CONT-CA01 Properties dialog box

5. Click the Properties button. The Properties dialog box is displayed.

6. Select the first option (Set The Certificate Request Status To Pending. The Administrator Must Explicitly Issue The Certificate), as shown in Figure 8-7, and click OK. You are prompted to restart Certificate Services.

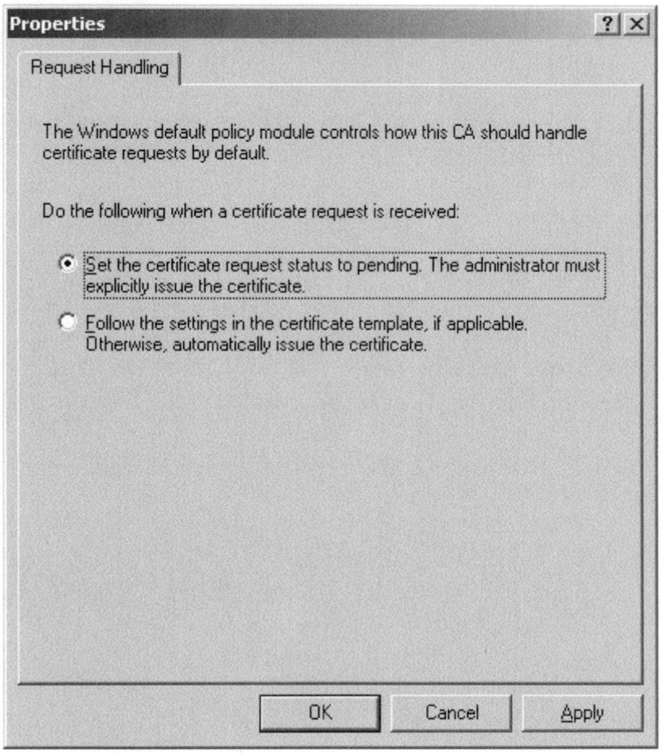

Figure 8-7
The Properties dialog box for the CONT-CA01 policy module

7. Click OK to close the prompt. Click OK to close the CONT-CA01 Properties dialog box and then close Certificate Authority.

8. Click Start>Administrative Tools>Services. Right-click the Certificate Services service and click Restart.

9. Close the Services console.

10. Stay logged on to Windows Server 2003 if you intend to complete Exercise 8.9.

Exercise 8.8	Renew a Certificate
Overview	You will renew a certificate on a client. Certificates are issued with an expiration date. When the certificates expire, a user will need to renew certificates if certificate autoenrollment is not enabled.
Completion time	5 minutes

 To complete Exercise 8.9, you should complete Exercise 8.7 before completing Exercise 8.8.

1. Still logged on to your Windows Vista client as sheelaw, click Start.

2. In the Start Search text box, key **certmgr.msc** and then press Enter. The Microsoft Management Console (MMC) is displayed with the Certificate Manager snap-in loaded.

3. In the Certificate Manager console, in the console tree, expand Personal and then select Certificates.

4. In the Details pane, right click the certificate issued to Sheela Word, point to All Tasks, and then click Renew Certificate With New Key. The Certificate Enrollment Wizard is displayed.

5. Click Next. The *Request Certificate* page is displayed.

6. Click Enroll. The certificate is renewed, and the *Certificate Installation Results* page is displayed. Click Finish.

7. Close the Certificate Manager snap-in.

Exercise 8.9   Approve a Certificate Request

Overview	You will review and approve pending certificate requests. When the Certificate Authority is configured to require administrator approval of certificate requests, an administrator must review and approve pending requests.
Completion time	5 minutes

 Complete Exercise 8.7 and Exercise 8.8 before starting this exercise.

1. If you are not already logged on to Windows Server 2003 as an administrator, log on to Windows Server 2003 with your administrator account (netadmin and p@ssw0rd).

2. Click Start>Administrative Tools>Certification Authority. The Certification Authority console is displayed. Expand the CONT-CA01 certification authority in the console tree.

3. Select Pending Requests. A list of Pending Requests is displayed in the Details pane, as shown in Figure 8-8.

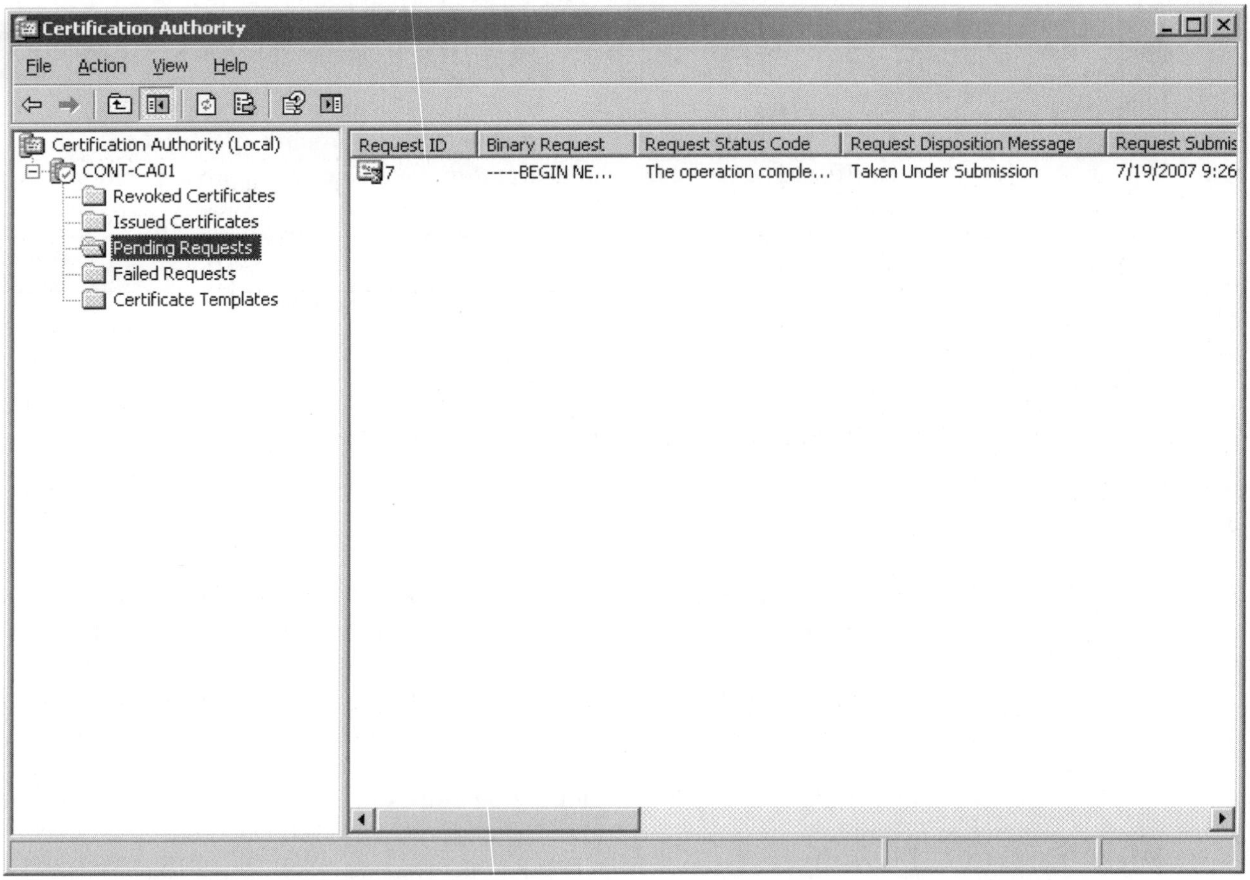

Figure 8-8
Pending requests in the Certification Authority

4. Right-click the pending certificate in the Details pane, point to All Tasks, and then click Issue. The certificate is issued.

5. Close the Certification Authority.

6. Log off of Windows Server 2003 and log off of the Windows Vista client.

LAB REVIEW QUESTIONS

Completion time   10 minutes

1.   What steps are required to share an encrypted file with another user?

2.   How can you roll out an encryption policy to multiple users? What if you want to require managers to encrypt certain documents, but allow other users to work without encryption?

3.   What tools can you use to manage a Certificate Authority?

LAB CHALLENGE: TURN ON BITLOCKER WITHOUT A TPM

Completion time   20 minutes

NOTE   *To complete this Lab Challenge, you will need a USB flash drive and a USB port on your Vista client. After you have completed this procedure, you will need the USB flash drive or the BitLocker Recovery password each time you start the client.*

Following the "Turn on BitLocker Without a TPM" procedure in Lesson 8 in the textbook, make sure you have enabled the Allow BitLocker Without A Compatible TPM Setting and then step through the BitLocker Drive Encryption process in the Control Panel. Keep notes about the steps required and provide them to your instructor.

LAB 9
CONFIGURING TASK SCHEDULER

This lab contains the following exercises and activities:

SCENARIO

You have decided to display a simple announcement on a particular Windows Vista client. You will use Task Scheduler to create the task to display the announcement. You will experiment with manipulating the task, including starting it, disabling it, enabling it, and editing it.

You also want to run a simple application on all clients every Thursday afternoon. (For this lab, you will use the MSPaint accessory.) To distribute a task to all clients, you will use Group Policy to configure a log-on script. Finally, you want to review information about when and why a task ran in the past.

After completing this lab, you will be able to:

- Use Task Scheduler to create a task.

- Disable or enable a task in Task Scheduler.

- Edit a task.

- Run a task on demand.

- Create a task by using the schtasks command-line utility.

- Configure log-on scripts through Group Policy.

- Distribute a task by using Group Policy and a log-on script.

Estimated lab time: 45 minutes

Exercise 9.1	Create a Task
Overview	You will create a task by using Task Scheduler. A user has asked you to generate a simple meeting reminder on her client. To create the reminder, you use Task Scheduler. The task simply displays a message every Thursday afternoon.
Completion time	10 minutes

1. With your server started, log on to your Windows Vista client as chrisa. To log on, key **contoso\chrisa** in the first box, key **p@ssw0rd** in the second box, and then press Enter.

2. Click Start. In the Start Search text box, key **Task Scheduler**. In the Programs list, click Task Scheduler. The Task Scheduler console is displayed.

3. In Task Scheduler, select Create Task in the Action menu. The Create Task dialog box is displayed, which—unlike the Create Basic Task Wizard—allows for full flexibility in constructing your task.

4. In the Create Task dialog box, on the General tab, key **Status Meeting Reminder** in the Name text box. Key **Reminder message** in the Description text box.

5. In the Create Task dialog box, select the Triggers tab and then click New. The New Trigger dialog box is displayed.

6. Select the Weekly option and set the time to 1:00:00 PM. Turn on the Thursday checkbox, as shown in Figure 9-1. Click OK.

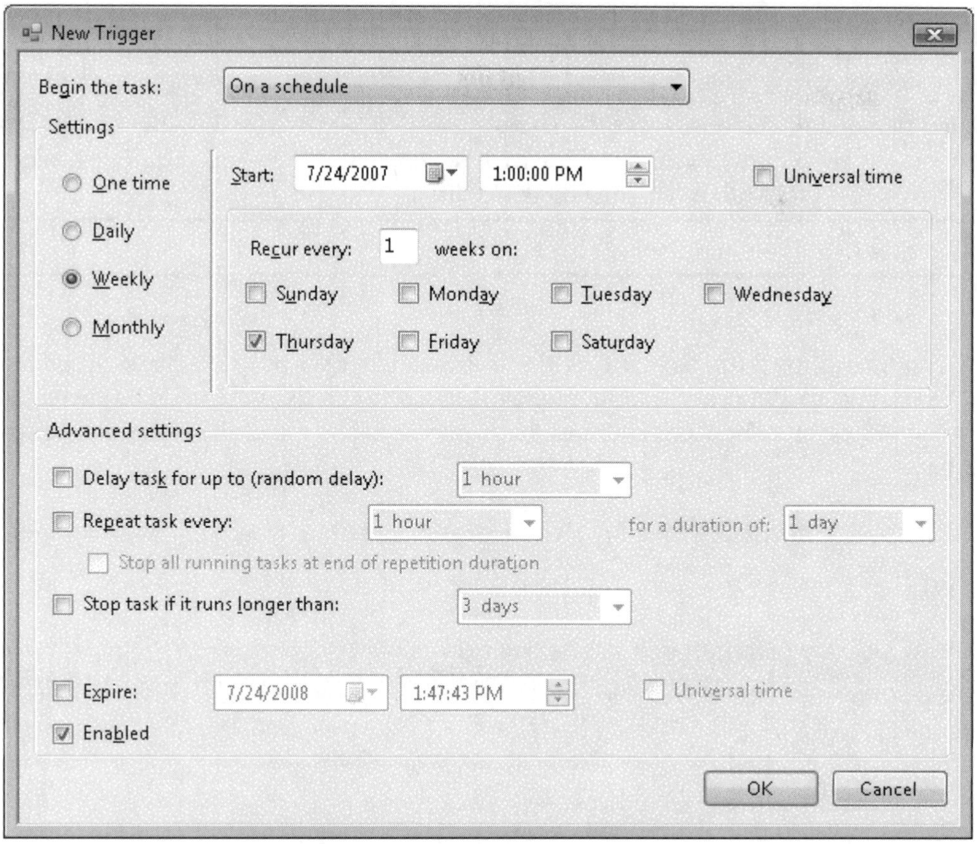

Figure 9-1
The New Trigger dialog box

7. In the Create Task dialog box, select the Actions tab and click New. The New Action dialog box is displayed.

8. Set the Action drop-down list to Display A Message. In the Title text box, key **Status Meeting**. In the Message text box, key **Please attend the Status Meeting at 1:30 in Room 123**. Click OK.

9. In the Create Task dialog box, click OK.

Question 1	What is the difference between choosing the Create Task and the Create Basic Task action?

Exercise 9.2	Start a Task
Overview	You will start a task in Task Scheduler. To test your meeting reminder, you will run it one time on demand.
Completion time	5 minutes

1. Continuing from Exercise 9.1, with Task Scheduler open, select Task Scheduler Library in the left pane and then click Refresh in the list of actions on the right. The Status Meeting Reminder task is displayed in the list at the top of the center pane.

2. Right-click the Status Meeting Reminder task and click Run, as shown in Figure 9-2.

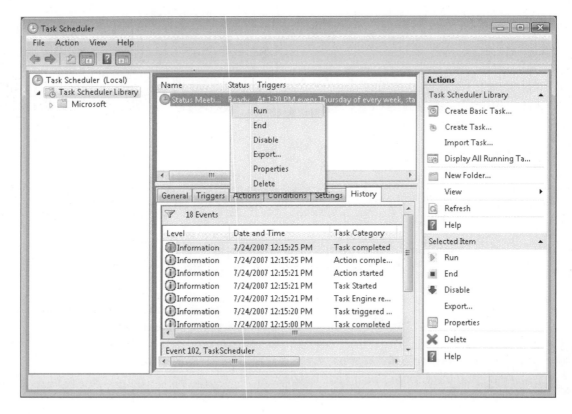

Figure 9-2
Running the Status Meeting Reminder task

3. Minimize the Task Scheduler to see the displayed Status Meeting message box, as shown in Figure 9-3.

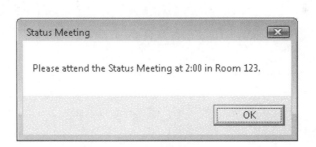

Figure 9-3
The Status Meeting message box

4. Click OK in the Status Meeting message box.

5. Click Task Scheduler in the Taskbar at the bottom of the Windows Vista desktop to display the Task Scheduler window.

Exercise 9.3	Disable, Enable, and Edit a Task
Overview	You will manipulate a task in Task Scheduler. Your user has asked you to show her how to turn the reminder on or off, and how to modify it if the message needs to be changed. You show her how to disable the task, enable the task, and change the text of the message.
Completion time	5 minutes

1. Continuing from Exercise 9.2 with the Task Scheduler open, right-click the Status Meeting Reminder task and click Disable.

2. Right-click the Status Meeting Reminder task again and notice that Run is no longer included in the context menu. Click Enable in the context menu.

3. Right-click the Status Meeting Reminder task again and click Properties. The Status Meeting Reminder Properties dialog box is displayed. This dialog box shows the same options as it displayed when creating a task in Exercise 9.1 and adds the History tab.

4. Select the Actions tab, select Display A Message in the Action list, and click Edit. The Edit Action dialog box is displayed.

5. Change the time in the Message text box from 1:30 to 2:00, as shown in Figure 9-4, and click OK.

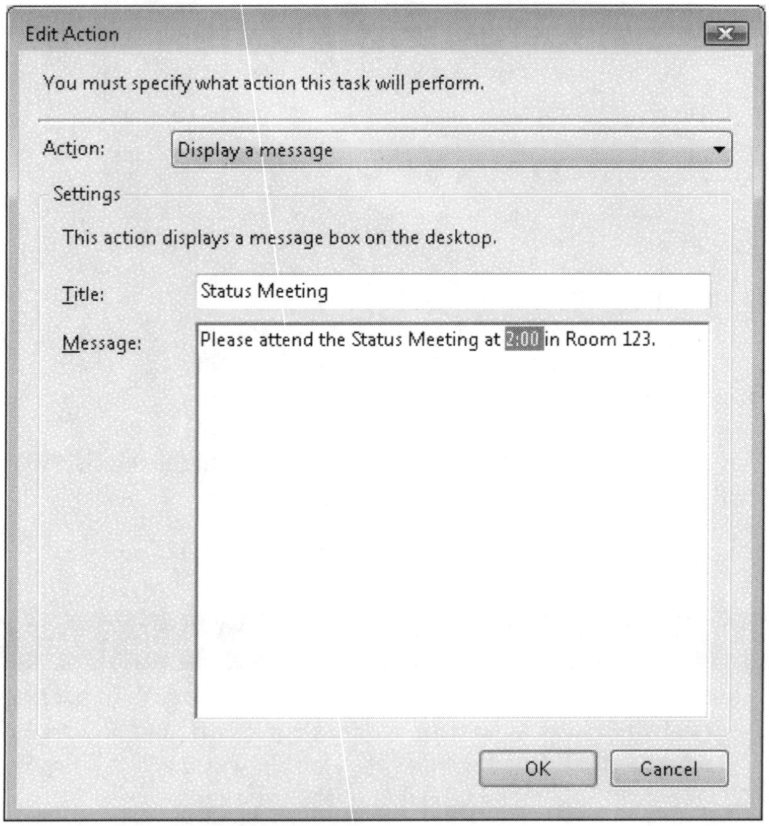

Figure 9-4
Editing the message displayed by a task

6. In the Status Meeting Reminder Properties dialog box, select the Triggers tab. Select the Weekly item in the Trigger list and click Edit. Change the start time from 1:00:00 PM to 1:30:00 PM. Click OK.

7. Click OK in the Status Meeting Reminder Properties dialog box.

Question 2	What aspects of a task are you able to edit?

Exercise 9.4	Distribute a Task
Overview	You will use Group Policy to distribute a task among many users. You need all your users to run a simple in-house application on a regular schedule. To implement a scheduled task across all clients, you have decided to create a log-on script. When each user logs on, the script will create a task on the user's client that will run a simple application at a scheduled time.
Completion time	20 minutes

Build a Script to Create a Task

1. Log on to Windows Server 2003 with your administrator account by keying **netadmin** in the User Name text box and keying **p@ssw0rd** in the Password text box.

2. Click Start>Windows Explorer. Windows Explorer opens. Expand My Computer in the Folders pane, then expand C:\Windows\SYSVOL\sysvol\contoso.com and select the scripts folder. This is the folder that is shared as \\WinSrv03\Netlogon.

 NOTE

Normally, you would build the following file while logged onto a client rather than directly on the server.

3. Right-click in the Details pane, point to New, and click Text Document. Key **PaintTaskScript.bat** and press Enter to rename the new document. The new file is shown highlighted in Figure 9-5. The Rename dialog box is displayed, asking whether you want to change the file name extension. Click Yes.

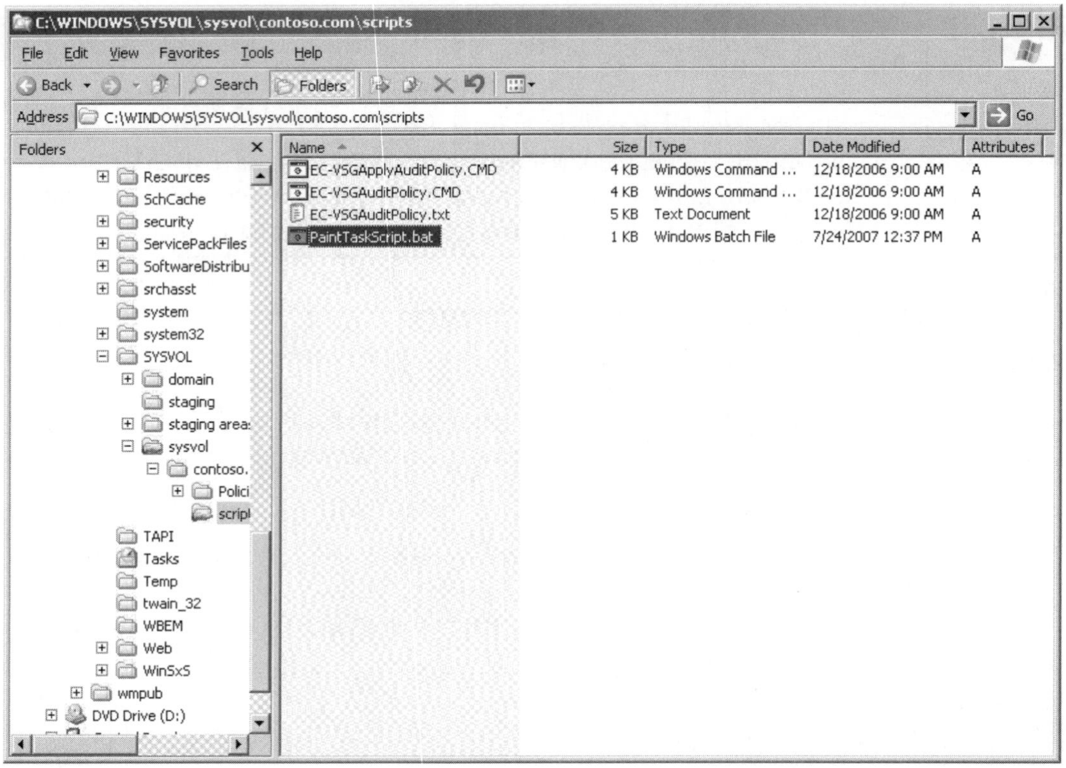
C:\WINDOWS\SYSVOL\sysvol\contoso.com\scripts
File Edit View Favorites Tools Help
Back Search Folders
Address C:\WINDOWS\SYSVOL\sysvol\contoso.com\scripts
Go
Folders
Resources
SchCache
security
ServicePackFiles
SoftwareDistribu
srchasst
system
system32
SYSVOL
domain
staging
staging area:
sysvol
contoso.
Polici
scripl
TAPI
Tasks
Temp
twain_32
WBEM
Web
WinSxS
wmpub
DVD Drive (D:)
Name Size Type Date Modified Attributes
EC-VSGApplyAuditPolicy.CMD 4 KB Windows Command ... 12/18/2006 9:00 AM A
EC-VSGAuditPolicy.CMD 4 KB Windows Command ... 12/18/2006 9:00 AM A
EC-VSGAuditPolicy.txt 5 KB Text Document 12/18/2006 9:00 AM A
PaintTaskScript.bat 1 KB Windows Batch File 7/24/2007 12:37 PM A

Figure 9-5
The new script in the Netlogon share

4. Right-click the PaintTaskScript.bat file and then click Edit. The Notepad window is displayed.

5. In Notepad, key **schtasks /Create /TN "Paint" /F /SC WEEKLY /D THU /ST 12:00 /TR mspaint**.

NOTE	*This exercise builds a task that runs the Paint accessory. Normally, you would replace mspaint with an in-house application you would like to run as a task.*

6. From the File menu, choose Save. Close Notepad.

7. Log off of the server.

Distribute the Task by Using Group Policy

8. Create a new GPO as instructed in Exercise 3.2, naming the new GPO Task Distribution GPO. Make sure the new GPO is linked and enabled as instructed in Exercise 3.2.

9. In the Group Policy Management console, right-click the Task Distribution GPO link under the contoso.com node and then select Edit. The Group Policy Object Editor console is displayed.

10. In the Group Policy Object Editor, in the console tree, expand User Configuration> Windows Settings and select Scripts (Logon/Logoff). In the Details pane, right-click the Logon policy and then click Properties. The Logon Properties dialog box is displayed.

11. Click Add. The Add a Script dialog box is displayed.

12. Key **WinSrv03\Netlogon\PaintTaskScript.bat** in the Script Name text box, as shown in Figure 9-6, and click OK.

Figure 9-6
The Add a Script dialog box

13. Click OK in the Logon Properties dialog box.

14. Close the Group Policy Object Editor console and the Group Policy Management console.

Test the Distributed Task

15. To test the task distribution, log off and log back on as chrisa. Click Start, key **Task Scheduler** in the Start Search box, and click Task Scheduler in the Programs list. The Task Scheduler window is displayed.

16. Select Task Scheduler Library in the left pane. The Details pane in the center now displays the Paint task. Right-click the Paint task and click Run. The Paint window is displayed, as shown in Figure 9-7.

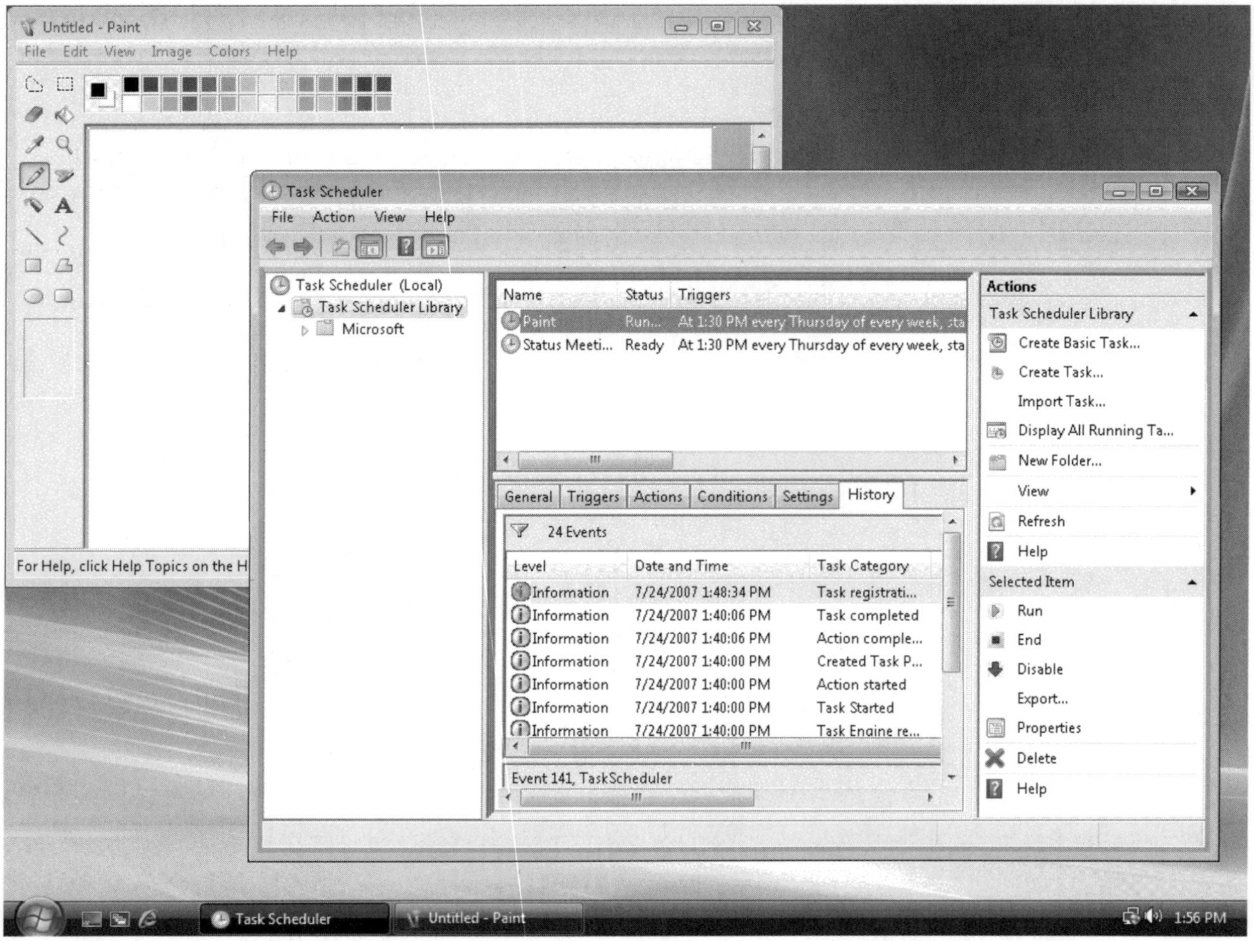

Figure 9-7
The Paint application, triggered by a task in Task Scheduler

17. Close the Paint window.

Question 3	What steps are required to distribute a task among many users?

Exercise 9.5	View Task History
Overview	You will review the history for a task in Task Scheduler. Task Scheduler provides a convenient log of information about a task. Its History tab includes information about the task's creation as well as when it ran, what caused it to run, and when and how the task completed. You need to review the history to troubleshoot any problems with a scheduled task.
Completion time	5 minutes

1. Continuing from Exercise 9.4, with Task Scheduler open, right-click the Paint task and click Properties. The Paint Properties dialog box is displayed.

2. Select the History tab. The History tab displays a list of the events involved each time the task ran, as shown in Figure 9-8.

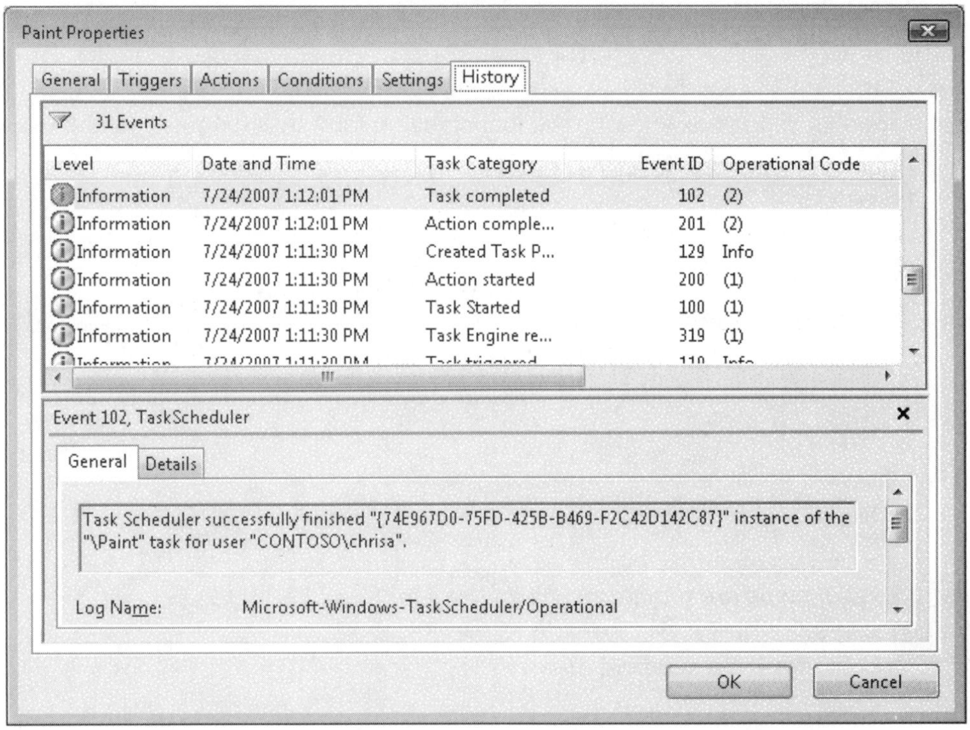

Figure 9-8
The History tab of the Paint Properties dialog box

3. Double-click any event to display the Event Properties dialog box, which gives additional information about the event. In Figure 9-9, which shows the launch event for the Paint task, note the Task Category is listed as Task Triggered By User. Figure 9-10 shows the launch event for the task when it is triggered by the time.

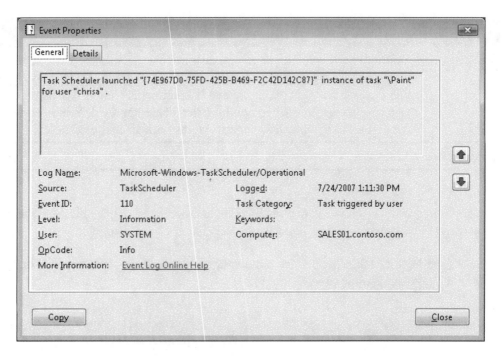

Figure 9-9
The Event Properties dialog box showing the launch event for a task triggered by the user

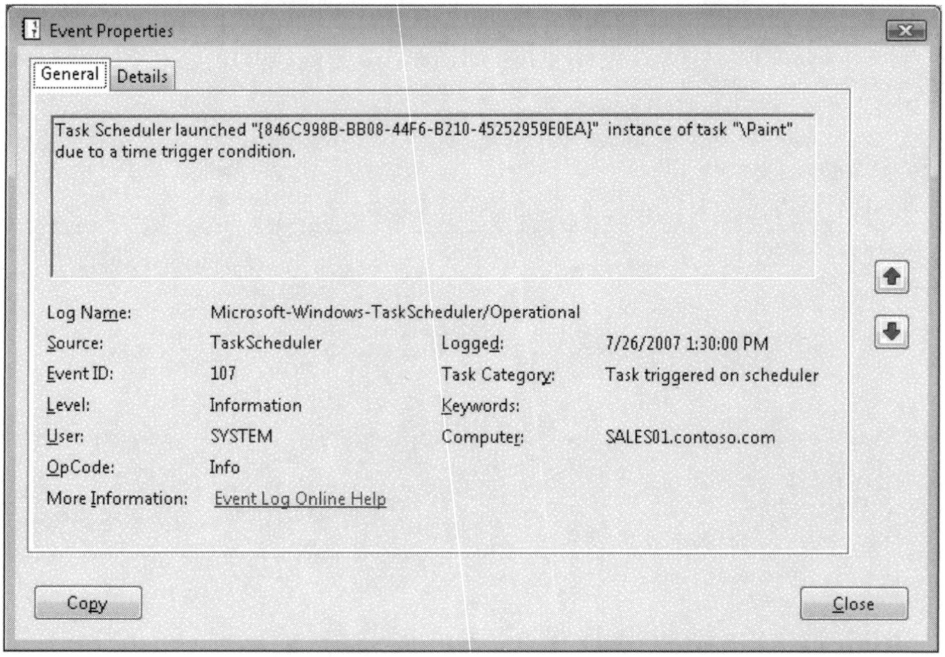

Figure 9-10
The Event Properties dialog box showing the launch event for a task triggered by a scheduled time

4. Close the Event Properties dialog box, the Paint Properties dialog box, and Task Scheduler, then log off of the client.

LAB REVIEW QUESTIONS

Completion time	10 minutes

1. After creating a task, how can you—without deleting or modifying the task—prevent the task from running?

2. When distributing a task, what intermediate tool is required? How do you create a new task for each user?

3. What are some types of task-related events that you can review on the History tab of the task's Properties dialog box?

LAB CHALLENGE: EXPORT AND IMPORT A TASK

Completion time	20 minutes

Use Task Scheduler to export a task to your desktop as an XML file. Using Notepad or any other editor, examine the resulting XML. Experiment with modifying some of the settings, including the task name, then import the task and review its properties. Print the updated XML file.

Also experiment with using the schtasks command-line utility. Create a task by using the /XML flag and the XML file to which you exported your task.

LAB 10
UPDATING VISTA

This lab contains the following exercises and activities:

SCENARIO

You have decided to manage the automatic updates for Windows Vista clients at Contoso. To distribute only approved updates to clients, you will run Windows Server Update Services (WSUS) on a server. The server will make available only those updates you want to deploy, and your Windows Vista clients will be configured to get their updates from the server rather than from the Windows Update Internet site.

Before making any particular update available, you will install the update on a test machine and analyze the resulting client configuration by using the Reliability and Performance Monitor as well as the Windows Diagnostic Infrastructure (WDI).

After completing this lab, you will be able to:

- Install WSUS.

- Configure a WSUS server.

- Configure clients to use a WSUS server.

- Select and deploy updates by using WSUS.

- Use the Reliability and Performance Monitor.

- Add counters in Performance Monitor.

- Open the Reliability Monitor.

- Configure Windows Diagnostic Infrastructure (WDI).

Estimated lab time: 65 minutes

Exercise 10.1	Install WSUS
Overview	You will install Windows Server Update Services (WSUS). You have decided to install WSUS with the default settings to distribute updates to clients from a local storage point. As you install WSUS, you note the folders and URLs that the installation wizard uses by default.
Completion time	25 minutes

Your server should already have the .NET Framework 2.0 installed. If not, download Microsoft .NET Framework Version 2.0 to your Windows Server 2003 machine from www.microsoft.com/downloads. After downloading the dotnetfx.exe file, run it and follow the on-screen prompts to install .NET Framework Version 2.0.

Your server should also have the Microsoft Report Viewer 2005 installed, available at www.microsoft.com/downloads. You need the Report Viewer to use the WSUS Administration UI, and you can install the Report Viewer after installing WSUS.

1. Log on to your Windows Server 2003 machine as an administrator (use netadmin and p@ssw0rd).

2. Download the Windows Server Update Services 3.0 setup file to your Windows Server 2003 machine from http://technet.microsoft.com.

<table>
<tr><td style="writing-mode: vertical">NOTE</td><td>*For this lab, you need to install only the components explicitly mentioned in the Exercise 10.1 procedure. For a full enterprise installation, configure the WSUS installation to match your needs, including partitioning your server's hard drive, changing your firewall settings, modifying IIS settings, and using an existing database engine instead of the default database engine. For details about configuring your WSUS installation, consult http://technet.microsoft.com.*</td></tr>
</table>

3. After downloading the WSUS3Setup file, run it to install WSUS 3.0. Follow the prompts on the screen for a full server installation, accepting all defaults. In particular, when prompted to select an update source, select the Store Updates Locally checkbox and verify that C:\WSUS appears in the corresponding text box. Note the URL, server name, and port number listed on the *Web Site Selection* page, as shown in Figure 10-1. You might also want to note the folders and URL listed on the *Ready To Install Windows Server Update Services 3.0* page. If the WSUS Configuration Wizard starts after the installation, cancel it; you will configure WSUS in subsequent steps.

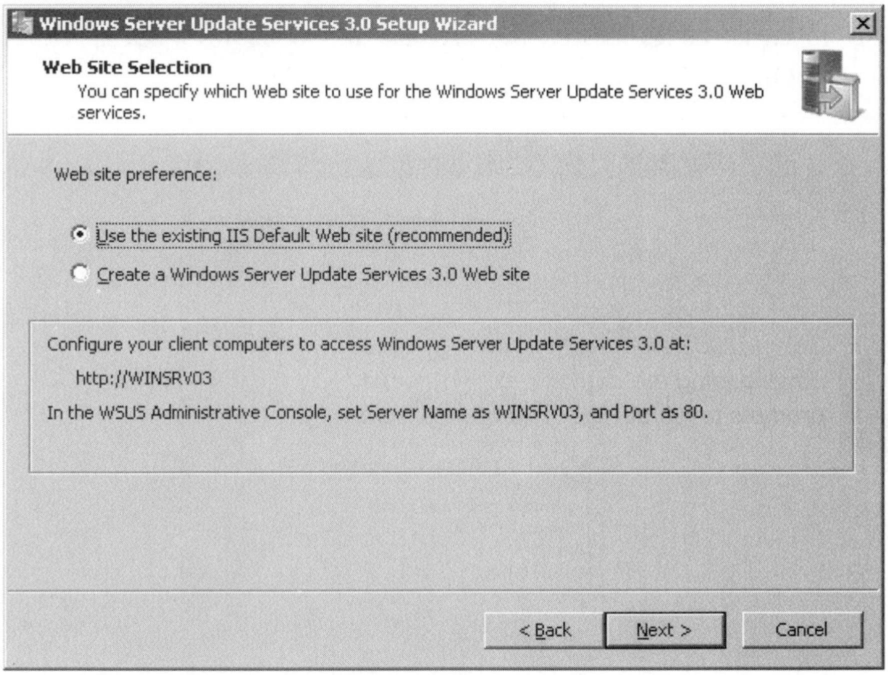

Figure 10-1
The *Web Site Selection* page of the WSUS installation wizard specifies the URL, website, and port number that you will use in configuring the clients and administering the server.

Exercise 10.2	Configure a WSUS Server
Overview	You will configure the WSUS server to download updates for Windows Vista clients. You have decided to use WSUS to automatically distribute critical, security, and definition updates for Windows Vista only. You configure the WSUS server, synchronize the available updates, and approve selected updates for distribution.
Completion time	20 minutes

1. On your Windows Server 2003 machine, click Start>All Programs>Administrative Tools>Microsoft Windows Server Update Services 3.0. The Update Services console is displayed.

2. In the console tree, expand WINSRV03. Select the Synchronizations node. In the Action menu, select Synchronize Now. This is necessary for the Products tab (which you'll deal with in subsequent steps) to display all the products. If the synchronization takes more than a few minutes to complete, you can click Stop Synchronization in the Actions list.

3. Select the Options node and then click the Products And Classifications link in the Options pane. The Products And Classifications dialog box is displayed.

4. Clear all check boxes and then select only the Windows Vista checkbox, as shown in Figure 10-2.

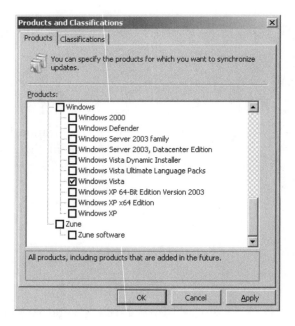

Figure 10-2
The Products And Classifications dialog box

5. Select the Classifications tab of the Products And Classifications dialog box. Verify that only the Critical Updates, Security Updates, and Definition Updates checkboxes are selected. Click OK.

6. Again, select the Synchronization node in the console tree. Click Synchronize Now in the Actions list. You can select the synchronization item in the Synchronizations list to see a progress indicator, as shown in Figure 10-3.

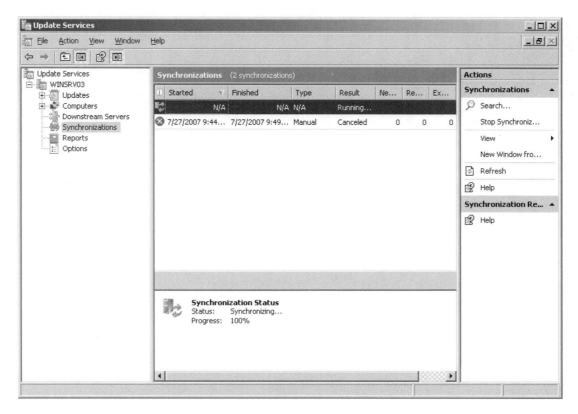

Figure 10-3
The synchronization progress indicator is displayed at the bottom of the Details pane

7. In the console tree, select WINSRV03 after synchronization is complete. A To Do list is displayed in the Details pane, as shown in Figure 10-4. Click the Approved link next to the number of critical updates waiting to be approved.

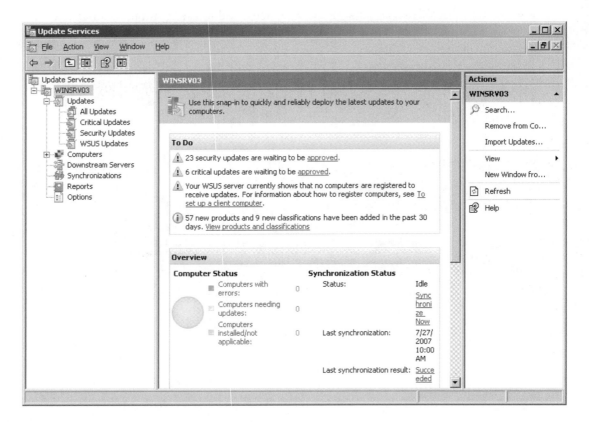

Figure 10-4
The To Do list tells you the number and type of updates waiting to be approved.

8. Right-click a recent update in the Critical Updates list and click Approve. (When you select an update, the update's release date is displayed in the Status section at the bottom of the Details pane.) The Approve Updates dialog box is displayed.

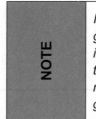

In WSUS you segregate clients in your enterprise by creating computer groups. If you have one or more test machines, you can segregate them into their own WSUS computer group, apply updates via WSUS, and then analyze the test machines before approving the updates for other machines in the enterprise. This lab uses the default All Computers group.

9. Click the down arrow for the All Computers group and choose Approved For Install, as shown in Figure 10-5. Click OK.

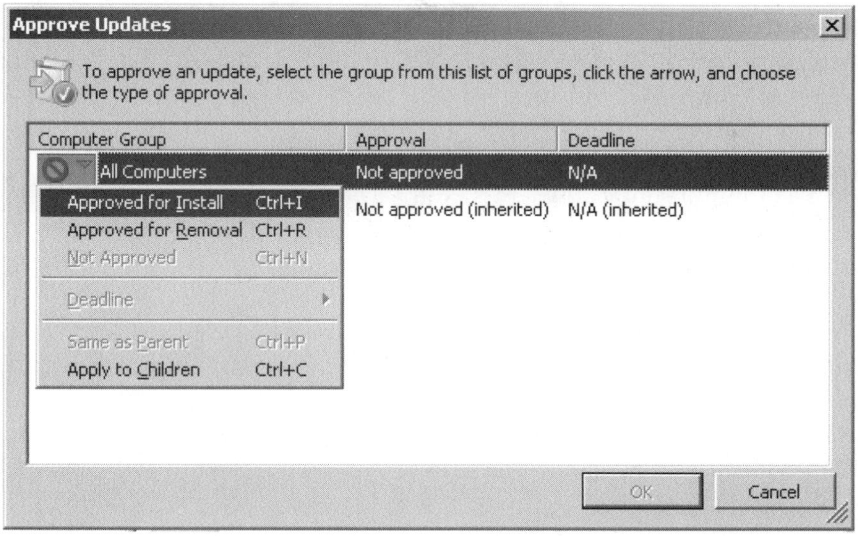

Figure 10-5
Approving an update in the Approve Updates dialog box

10. An Approval Progress dialog box displays the progress of the approval. Click the Close button.

11. Close the WSUS console and log off of the server.

Question 1	*Does WSUS apply to software other than versions of the Windows operating system? Hint: examine the Products tab of the Products And Classifications option in the WSUS console.*

Exercise 10.3   Configure WSUS Clients

Overview	You will configure a client to download updates from the WSUS server. You want to configure your Windows Vista clients to check your WSUS server nightly for new updates to install.
Completion time	10 minutes

Configure the Client

1. Log on to your Windows Vista client as chrisa. (If the log-on screen displays contoso\chrisa, you can simply key **p@ssw0rd** in the Password box and then press Enter.)

2. Create a new GPO as instructed in Exercise 3.2, giving the new GPO the name WSUS GPO. Make sure the new GPO is linked and enabled as instructed in Exercise 3.2.

3. In the Group Policy Management console, right-click the WSUS GPO link under the contoso.com node and then select Edit. The Group Policy Object Editor console is displayed.

4. In the Group Policy Object Editor console tree, expand Computer Configuration>Administrative Templates>Windows Components. Then select Windows Update.

5. In the Details pane, right-click Configure Automatic Updates and then click Properties. The Configure Automatic Updates Properties dialog box is displayed.

6. Select Enabled. In the Configure Automatic Updating drop-down list, select 4 - Auto Download And Schedule The Install, as shown in Figure 10-6. Click OK.

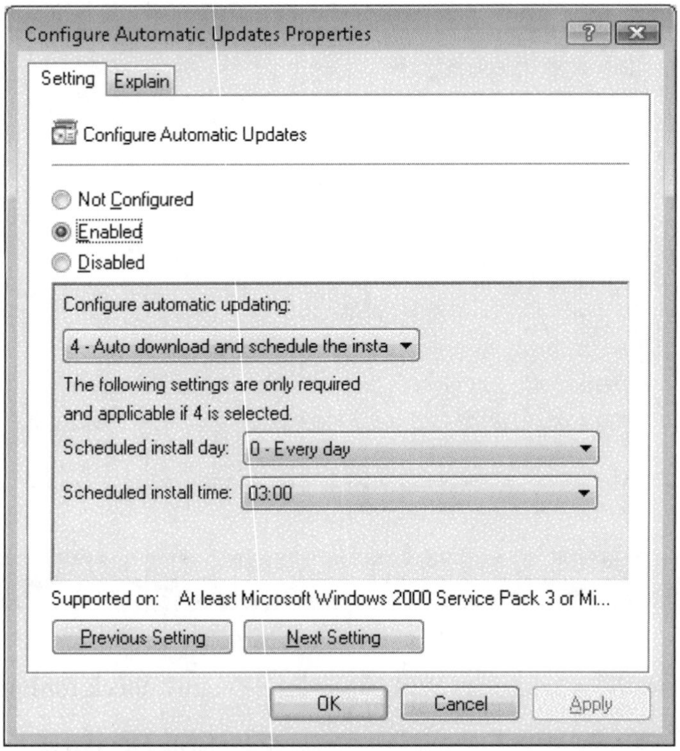

Figure 10-6
The Configure Automatic Updates Properties dialog box

7. In the Details pane, right-click Specify Intranet Microsoft Update Service Location and then click Properties. The Specify Intranet Microsoft Update Service Location Properties dialog box appears.

8. Select Enabled. In the Set The Intranet Update Service For Detecting Updates text box, key **http://WINSRV03** (as noted in Figure 10-1). In the Set The Intranet Statistics Server text box, again key **http://WINSRV03**. Click OK.

9. In the Details pane, right-click Automatic Updates Detection Frequency and then click Properties. The Automatic Updates Detection Frequency Properties dialog box is displayed.

10. Select Enabled and click OK.

11. In the Details pane, right-click Reschedule Automatic Updates Scheduled Installations and then click Properties. The Reschedule Automatic Updates Scheduled Installations Properties dialog box is displayed.

12. Select Enabled and click OK.

13. In the Details pane, right-click Enabling Windows Update Power Management To Automatically Wake Up The System To Install Scheduled Updates and then click Properties. The Enabling Windows Update Power Management To Automatically Wake Up The System To Install Scheduled Updates Properties dialog box is displayed.

14. Select Enabled and click OK.

Set Windows Firewall to Allow the WSUS Server

15. To prevent Windows Firewall settings from interfering with Windows Update, in the Group Policy Management console, right-click the Firewall GPO that you created in Lab 7, "Using Windows Firewall and Windows Defender." If the Link Enabled menu option has a checkmark next to it, click the Link Enabled option to disable the GPO link.

> *In a real-life setting, instead of disabling the Firewall GPO you would configure your Group Policy to allow http://WINSRV03 as a Windows Update Website in Windows Firewall.*

Test the Configuration

To test the client's connection to the WSUS server, manually check for updates.

16. Click Start. In the Start Search box, key **gpupdate** and press Enter.

17. Click Start>Control Panel. Under Security, click the Check For Updates link.

18. Click the Check For Updates button. The Control Panel displays a progress bar, as shown in Figure 10-7.

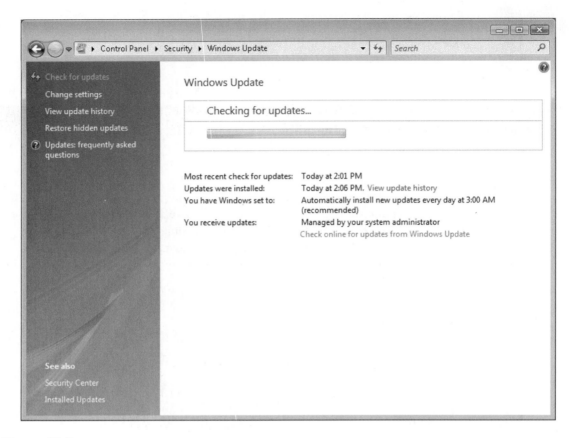

Figure 10-7
Progress bar displayed

19. You might be prompted to install new Windows Update software before checking for updates. If so, click the Install Now button and enter your administrator credentials (netadmin and p@ssw0rd) if prompted. Depending on how your client was installed and when it was last updated, Windows Update might tell you that Windows is up-to-date, or it might prompt you to install available updates. Either outcome tells you that your client is properly communicating with the WSUS server. (To be certain the client is communicating with the server, rather than with the Windows Update site, you can also click Change Settings on the Windows Update section of Control Panel. The Change Settings section of Control Panel includes a yellow bar near the top stating "Some settings are managed by your system administrator," which indicates that your Group Policy settings have been applied.) If an update is installed, you might also be prompted to restart your machine.

When you select an update in the Update Services console on your WSUS server, the Details pane in the console displays pie-chart graphs indicating the number of computers needing specific updates as well as the number of computers on which the update is already installed.

Question 2	How does Windows Firewall interact with WSUS? What does Windows Update require with respect to Windows Firewall to download updates?

Exercise 10.4   Use the Reliability and Performance Monitor

Overview	You will examine performance counters and reliability statistics. After updating a test machine, you can analyze the machine to make sure it is performing properly before deploying the same set of updates throughout the enterprise. As part of your analysis, you will check performance counters in the Performance Monitor to see how a machine is currently running. You will also examine the Reliability Monitor to see whether the updates have caused any failures since being installed.
Completion time	5 minutes

1. Still logged on to your Windows Vista client as chrisa, click Start. In the Start Search text box, key **perfmon.msc** and then press Ctrl + Shift + Enter. A User Account Control dialog box is displayed.

2. Provide administrator credentials (netadmin and p@ssw0rd) and then click OK. The Reliability And Performance Monitor is displayed.

3. In the console tree, expand Monitoring Tools and then select Performance Monitor.

4. In the Details pane, click the green plus sign in the menu bar at the top. The Add Counters dialog box is displayed.

5. Click the down arrow next to Memory in the list and then select % Committed Bytes In Use in the list, as shown in Figure 10-8. Click the Add button. You can experiment with adding other counters, hiding a counter, highlighting a counter, removing counters, and so forth.

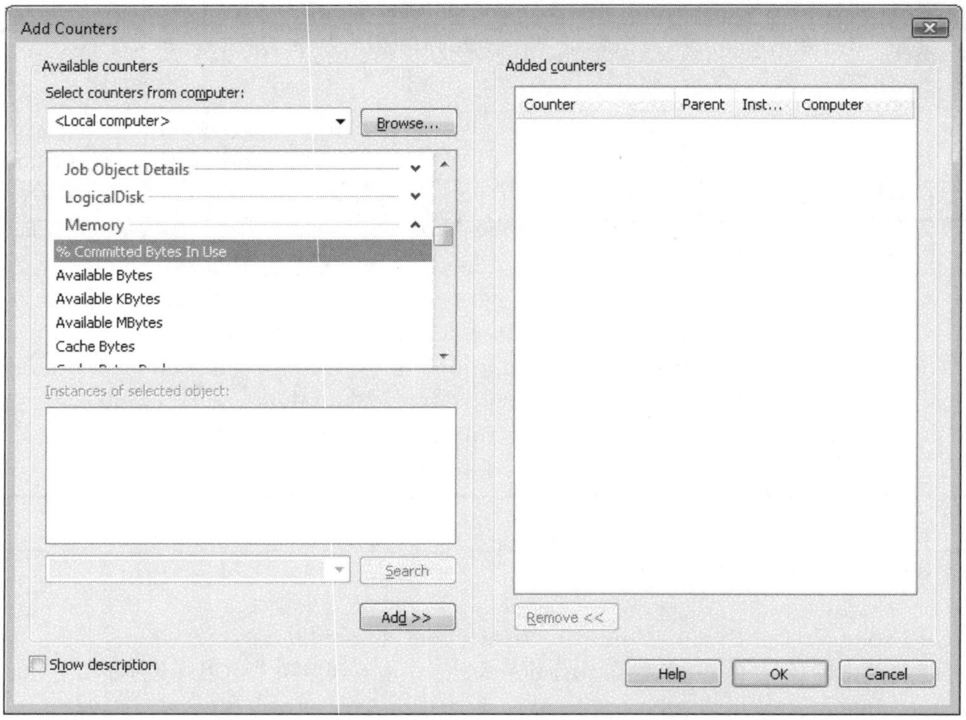

Figure 10-8
Adding a memory performance counter

6. In the console tree, select Reliability Monitor. The Reliability Monitor is displayed. If you had any failures, they will be highlighted on the System Stability Chart.

7. Close the Reliability And Performance Monitor and log off of the Windows Vista client.

Question 3	*Explain what you can check in Performance Monitor as opposed to what you can check using the Reliability Monitor.*

Exercise 10.5	Configure WDI
Overview	You will configure Windows Diagnostic Infrastructure (WDI) by using Group Policy. You want clients to recover—without requiring user intervention—from any file corruption that might occur. You establish a Group Policy to allow file corruption recovery to proceed silently.
Completion time	5 minutes

1. Still logged on to your Windows Vista client as chrisa, create a new GPO as instructed in Exercise 3.2, giving the new GPO the name WDI GPO. Make sure the new GPO is linked and enabled as instructed in Exercise 3.2.

2. In the Group Policy Management console, right-click the WDI GPO link under the contoso.com node and then select Edit. The Group Policy Object Editor console is displayed.

3. Expand Computer Configuration>Administrative Templates>System> Troubleshooting And Diagnostics. Then select Corrupted File Recovery.

4. In the Details pane, right-click Configure Corrupted File Recovery Behavior and click Properties. The Configure Corrupted File Recovery Behavior Properties dialog box is displayed.

5. Select Enabled and then select Silent in the Scenario Execution Level drop-down list, as shown in Figure 10-9. Click OK.

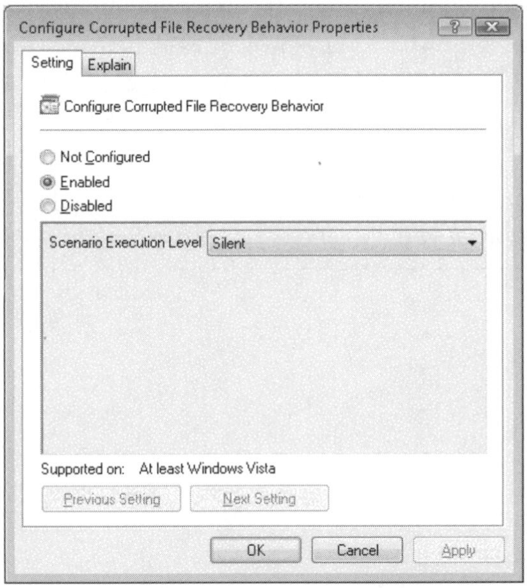

Figure 10-9
The Configure Corrupted File Recovery Behavior Properties dialog box

LAB REVIEW QUESTIONS

Completion time	10 minutes

1. If you want to approve updates before deploying them, what are the major steps in configuring a WSUS server?

2. After configuring the WSUS server, what else must you do to distribute updates to clients? What tools can you use to accomplish this additional task?

3. The Reliability And Performance Monitor lets you examine a system for problems. What tool automatically monitors system performance and takes corrective action if necessary?

LAB CHALLENGE: USE TOOLS IN THE ADVANCED TOOLS SECTION OF CONTROL PANEL

Completion time	10 minutes

Open the Advanced Tools section of Control Panel. Use the tools in this control panel to view performance-related events and system information. Press the PrtScr key to capture an image of the tools you use and save the images on the server in the following location: \\winsrv03\Redirect\Pictures\AdvancedToolsXX.bmp. (Your instructor might specify an alternate location with subfolders for each student.)

LAB 11

UNDERSTANDING, CONFIGURING, AND SECURING TCP/IP NETWORKS

This lab contains the following exercises and activities:

SCENARIO

One of the employees at Contoso is having network connectivity problems. You begin troubleshooting the machine by manually changing the network IP addresses for the machine by using known available IP addresses. You then change the network settings to obtain IP addresses automatically. Because the employee sometimes takes the machine home, you also set the machine to use Automatic Private Internet Protocol Addressing (APIPA) to find an appropriate alternate IP address when disconnected from the Contoso network.

You also decide to use Group Policy to establish overall authentication policies throughout the enterprise. On a particular machine, you will test implementing a more restrictive security authentication policy that requires inbound authentication when connecting to DNS servers, but only when the machine is connected to the domain.

After completing this lab, you will be able to:

- Configure IPv4 TCP/IP settings.

- Hard-code IP addresses in TCP/IP network settings.

- Configure network settings to automatically obtain IP addresses from a DHCP server.

- Use Group Policy to configure Wired Network security policies.

- Use Windows Firewall with Advanced Security to create IPSec rules.

Estimated lab time: 55 minutes

Exercise 11.1	Configure IPv4 TCP/IP Network Settings Manually
Overview	You will hard-code IP addresses in a client's network settings. An employee is experiencing trouble connecting to the network. To rule out problems with IP addresses, you will set the client's IP address using a known available address, and you will hard-code the address for the enterprise DNS server. Before changing these network settings, you record the existing settings for future reference.
Completion time	10 minutes

1. With your server started, log on to your Windows Vista client as chrisa. To log on, key **contoso\chrisa** in the first box, key **p@ssw0rd** in the second box, and then press Enter.

2. Click Start and then click Control Panel. Control Panel is displayed.

3. Under Network and Internet, click View Network Status And Tasks. The Network And Sharing Center control panel is displayed.

4. Click Manage Network Connections in the task list. The Network Connections control panel is displayed.

5. Right-click Local Area Connection for contoso.com and then click Properties, as shown in Figure 11-1. A User Account Control dialog box is displayed.

Figure 11-1
The Local Area Connection for contoso.com in the Network Connections control panel

6.   Provide administrator credentials (netadmin and p@ssw0rd) and then click OK. The Local Area Connection Properties dialog box is displayed.

7.   In the This Connection Uses The Following Items list box, select Internet Protocol Version 4 (TCP/IPv4) and then click Properties. The Internet Protocol Version 4 (TCP/IPv4) Properties dialog box is displayed.

> *Appropriate settings for the IP address, subnet mask, default gateway, Preferred DNS server, and especially the Alternate DNS server will depend on your lab environment, and they may have already been set up for your installation. If you change these settings, record the existing settings so you can restore them as part of the lab clean-up.*

8.   Select the Use The Following IP Address option. (If this option is already selected and this section has entries, record the existing settings before proceeding.) In the IP Address section, key **192.168.1.201**. In the Subnet Mask section, key **255.255.255.0**. In the Default Gateway section, key **192.168.1.1**, which should match your router's IP address.

9.   Select the Use The Following DNS Server Addresses option. (If this option is already selected and this section has entries, record the existing settings before proceeding.) In the Preferred DNS Server section, key **192.168.1.200**, which should match the IP address of your WinSrv03 machine. In the Alternate DNS server section, to have Internet connectivity, key the IP address for your Internet Service Provider (ISP).

> *Normally, the Use The Following DNS Server Addresses option is not selected in an enterprise environment.*

10.   Click OK to close the Internet Protocol Version 4 (TCP/IPv4) Properties dialog box.

11.   Click Close to close the Local Area Connection Properties dialog box.

12.   Leave the Network Connections control panel open and continue to Exercise 11.2.

Exercise 11.2	Use DHCP to Configure IPv4 TCP/IP Settings Automatically
Overview	You will change the client's network settings to obtain IP addresses automatically. You reset the client machine to obtain the client IP address and the IP address for the DNS server automatically.
Completion time	10 minutes

1. Continuing from the final step in the previous exercise, in the Network Connections control panel, right-click Local Area Connection for contoso.com and then click Properties. A User Account Control dialog box is displayed.

> **NOTE**
>
> *If the Network Connections control panel is not open, repeat Step 1 through Step 4 of the previous exercise.*

2. Provide administrator credentials (netadmin and p@ssw0rd) and then click OK. The Local Area Connection Properties dialog box is displayed.

3. In the This Connection Uses The Following Items list box, select Internet Protocol Version 4 (TCP/IPv4) and then click Properties. The Internet Protocol Version 4 (TCP/IPv4) Properties dialog box is displayed.

> **NOTE**
>
> *Appropriate settings for the IP address, subnet mask, default gateway, Preferred DNS server, and the Alternate DNS server will depend on your lab environment, and may have already been set up for your installation. If you change these settings,record the existing settings so you can restore them as part of the lab clean-up.*

4. Select the Obtain An IP Address Automatically option. Also select the Obtain DNS Server Address Automatically option. (Select this option if your DNS servers provide at least one DNS server as part of dynamic host control protocol (DHCP) options.)

5. Click OK to close the Internet Protocol Version 4 (TCP/IPv4) Properties dialog box.

6. Click Close to close the Local Area Connection Properties dialog box.

7. Leave the Network Connections control panel open and continue to Exercise 11.3.

Question 1	*If you modify network settings, what simple precaution should you take so that you can restore previous settings?*

Exercise 11.3	Configure an Alternate IP Address
Overview	You will set the client to obtain an APIPA address when not connected to the enterprise network. The client (a laptop) is sometimes used at home, connected to the employee's home network. To allow network connectivity with both networks, you configure an alternate IP address. Because you don't know the exact setup for the home network, you configure the machine to find an APIPA address if the domain is not available.
Completion time	10 minutes

1. Continuing from Exercise 11.2, in the Internet Protocol Version 4 (TCP/IPv4) Properties dialog box, verify that Obtain An IP Address Automatically is selected and then click the Alternate Configuration tab.

2. Select the Automatic Private IP Address option to use an APIPA address when the client is connected to an alternate network.

It is preferable to select the User Configured option and specify actual IP addresses to match the home network to which the client will connect. Otherwise, when an APIPA address is assigned, the DHCP client in Vista continues to send out DHCPDISCOVER messages.

3. Click OK to close the Internet Protocol Version 4 (TCP/IPv4) Properties dialog box.

4. Click Close to close the Local Area Connection Properties dialog box.

5. Close the Network Connections control panel. Close the Network control panel.

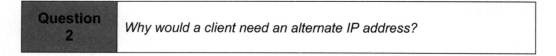

Question 2	*Why would a client need an alternate IP address?*

Lab Cleanup	Restore Network Settings
Overview	You will restore the recorded system settings before proceeding to Exercise 11.4.

Repeat steps 1–7 of Exercise 11.1 and then use the recorded settings to restore—to their original values—all settings you changed.

Exercise 11.4	Configure Windows Vista Wired Network Policy Through Group Policy
Overview	You will configure network policies by using Group Policy. Rather than configure each client individually, configure network settings throughout the enterprise by updating settings in a single location. Group Policy enables you to configure network settings for a group of clients and to later deploy updates as necessary from a single source. You have decided to use this method to force all clients that connect through a wired network to use a particular form of authentication and to prevent clients from caching user information.
Completion time	15 minutes

1. Still logged on to your Windows Vista client as chrisa, create a new GPO as instructed in Exercise 3.2, giving the new GPO the name WiredNet GPO. Make sure the new GPO is linked and enabled as instructed in Exercise 3.2.

> *You can configure only one wired network policy in the Wired Network (IEEE 802.3) Policies Group Policy node. You can, however, configure a wired and a wireless network policy in a single Group Policy. The wireless network policy node is Wireless Network (IEEE 802.11) Policies and the node can have a Vista and an XP setting.*

2. In the Group Policy Management console, right-click the WiredNet GPO link under the contoso.com node and then select Edit. The Group Policy Object Editor console is displayed.

3. In the Group Policy Object Editor console tree, expand Computer Configuration>Windows Settings>Security Settings. Then right-click Wired Network (IEEE 802.3) Policies and click Create A New Windows Vista Policy. The New Vista Wired Network Policy Properties dialog box is displayed.

Your lab environment should already have the appropriate Active Directory schema extensions installed. However, if a Wired Network Policy Management dialog box is displayed indicating that a newer version of the Active Directory schema may be required, refer to http://technet.microsoft.com for information about extending the Active Directory schema for wired and wireless networking.

4. In the Policy Name text box, key **Vista Wired Network Policy**. In the Description text box, key **PEAP authentication with no caching**.

5. Verify that the Use Windows Wired Auto Config Service For Clients checkbox is selected.

6. Click the Security tab. In the Select A Network Authentication Method drop-down list, select Protected EAP (PEAP). Click the Properties button. The Protected EAP Properties dialog box is displayed.

7. Select the CONT-CA01 certification authority in the Trusted Root Certification Authorities list. Verify that the Enable Fast Reconnect checkbox is selected, as shown in Figure 11-2. Click OK.

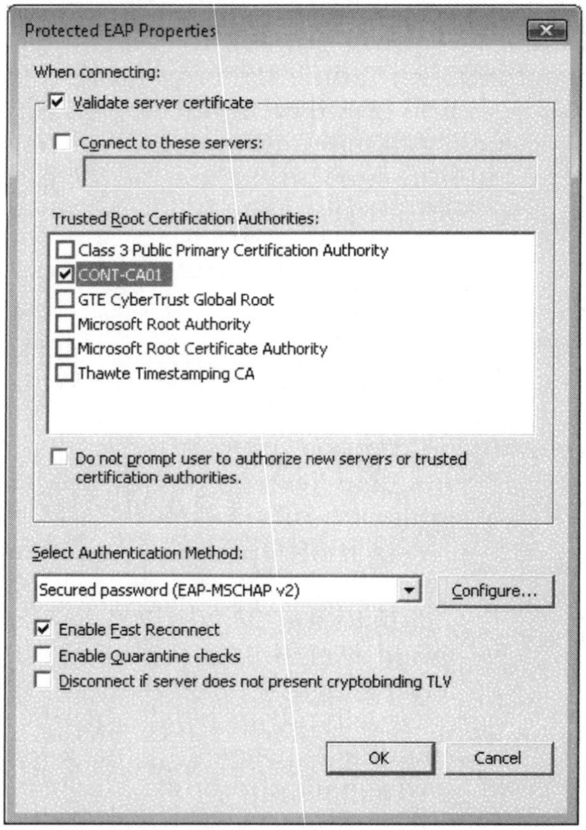

Figure 11-2
The Protected EAP Properties dialog box

8. In the Authentication Mode drop-down list, select User Re-authentication. Clear the Cache User Information For Subsequent Connections To This Network checkbox. Click OK.

9. Close the Group Policy Object Editor console and the Group Policy Management console.

Exercise 11.5	Create an IPsec Rule by Using Windows Firewall with Advanced Security
Overview	You will configure a custom IPsec rule. IPsec (Internet Protocol security) is a protocol suite that secures communications among machines by requiring authentication. You would like to implement a more restrictive security authentication policy that requires inbound authentication when connecting to DNS servers, but only when the machine is connected to the domain. Before implementing your new policy across the enterprise, test the custom rule on a particular machine. You will use Windows Firewall with Advanced Security to establish the rules that IPsec will enforce.
Completion time	10 minutes

1. Click Start. In the Start Search text box, key **Windows Firewall**. Right-click Windows Firewall With Advanced Security in the Programs list and then click Run As Administrator. A User Account Control dialog box is displayed.

2. Provide administrator credentials (netadmin and p@ssw0rd) and then click OK. The Windows Firewall with Advanced Security snap-in is displayed.

3. In the console tree, select Connection Security Rules, right-click Connection Security Rules, and then click New Rule. The *Rule Type* page of the New Connection Security Rule Wizard is displayed.

4. Select Custom and then click Next. The *Endpoints* page is displayed.

5. Under Which Computers Are In Endpoint 1, select Any IP Address. Click Customize. The Customize Interface Types dialog box is displayed.

6. Select the These Interface Types option and then select the Local Area Network item in the list, as shown in Figure 11-3. Click OK.

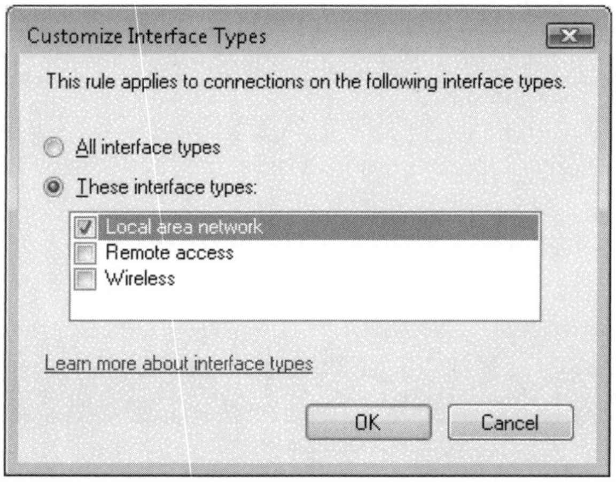

Figure 11-3
The Customize Interface Types dialog box

7. On the Endpoints page, under Which Computers Are In Endpoint 2, select the These IP Addresses option. Click the Add button. The IP Address dialog box is displayed.

8. Select the Predefined Set Of Computers option and then select DHCP Servers from the drop-down list, as shown in Figure 11-4. Click OK.

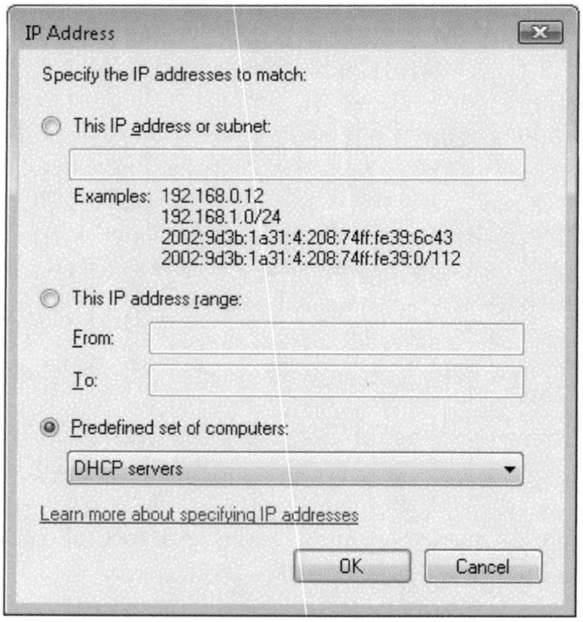

Figure 11-4
The IP Address dialog box

9. On the *Endpoints* page, click Next. The *Requirements* page is displayed.

10. Select the Require Authentication For Inbound Connections And Request Authentication For Outbound Connections option. This option will *require* that inbound traffic be authenticated, but will only *request* that outbound traffic be authenticated.

11. Click Next. The *Authentication Method* page is displayed.

12. Select the Computer And User (Kerberos V5) option to require authentication of both the host and the user by using Kerberos V5. Click Next. The Profile page is displayed.

13. Verify that the Domain checkbox is selected, but clear both the Private checkbox and the Public checkbox. Click Next. The *Name* page is displayed.

14. In the Name text box, key **Inbound authentication on domain connections**.

15. In the Description (Optional) text box, key **Require inbound authentication for computer and user when connected to the domain**.

16. Click Finish. The rule is added to the Connection Security Rules list.

17. Close the Windows Firewall With Advanced Security console and log off of the client.

LAB REVIEW QUESTIONS

Completion time   10 minutes

1. What tools do you use to manage network connections on an individual client? What tools can you use to manage network connections throughout the enterprise?

2. In what way does Group Policy limit wired network policies? Can you have multiple network policies in a single Group Policy Object?

3. What aspect of network security does IPsec oversee? Why is it important?

LAB CHALLENGE: CONFIGURE WIRELESSS NETWORKING IN GROUP POLICY

Completion time   20 minutes

 Virtual PC does not support wireless networking. If you are using Virtual PC as your lab environment, you can still configure Group Policy as if a wireless network were being implemented, but you will not be able to test an actual wireless connection.

Create a new GPO and use the Computer Configuration>Windows Settings>Security Settings>Wireless Network (IEEE 802.11) Policies node in your GPO to configure settings for Windows Vista clients in a wireless network. Export your policy as an XML file by clicking the Export button on the General tab of the wireless policy's Properties dialog box. Save the file in the \\winsrv03\Redirect\Pictures folder as WirelessPolicy.xml. Your instructor might specify an alternate location, possibly with subfolders for each student.

LAB 12
CONFIGURING AND TROUBLESHOOTING ACCESS

This lab contains the following exercises and activities:

SCENARIO

You want all users at Contoso to be able to receive the best level of support from your help desk, so you will make Remote Assistance possible for all employees. Further, you would like users to be able to connect remotely to their work machines from home by using the Remote Desktop facility. You also must troubleshoot a problem an employee is having with a redirected desktop file by checking the user's effective permissions on the folder.

In addition, Contoso's management wants employees in the marketing department to work from home without connecting directly to their workstations in the office. To enable employees to connect to the enterprise network from home, you permit dial-in access for certain employees, allow the Mktg user group to access the enterprise Virtual Private Network (VPN), and then have users configure their home machines to connect to the VPN. You can use Windows Network Diagnostics to diagnose any problems with the network connections.

After completing this lab, you will be able to:

- Set up Remote Assistance by using Group Policy.

- Set up Remote Desktop by using Group Policy.

- Troubleshoot file and folder permission problems.

- Allow dial-in access for a user.

- Allow users within a group to connect to a VPN.

- Set up a VPN connection on a client machine.

- Run the Windows Network Diagnostics utility.

Estimated lab time: 50 minutes

If you are using Virtual PC, the cumulative settings through the end of Lab 12 can cause your virtual server to run very slowly. It is recommended that you revert the client and server to an earlier virtual machine state (such as their state at the end of Lab 7) to increase performance while completing this lab.

Exercise 12.1	Configure Remote Assistance Through Group Policy
Overview	You will use Group Policy to enable Remote Assistance throughout the enterprise. You want all users at Contoso to have the option of receiving Remote Assistance from the corporate help desk. To allow Remote Assistance globally, use Group Policy to turn on the necessary settings.
Completion time	10 minutes

1. With your server started, log on to your Windows Vista client as chrisa. (If the logon screen displays contoso\chrisa, you can simply key **p@ssw0rd** in the Password box and then press Enter.)

2. Create a new GPO as instructed in Exercise 3.2, giving the new GPO the name Remote GPO. Ensure that the new GPO is linked and enabled as instructed in Exercise 3.2.

3. In the Group Policy Management console, right-click the Remote GPO link under the contoso.com node and then select Edit. The Group Policy Object Editor console is displayed.

4. Expand Computer Configuration>Administrative Templates>System. Then select the Remote Assistance node.

5. Right-click the Solicited Remote Assistance setting in the Details pane and click Properties. The Solicited Remote Assistance Properties dialog box is displayed.

6. Select the Enabled option. In the Method For Sending E-mail Invitations list select Simple MAPI. Click OK.

7. In the Group Policy Object Editor console, right-click the Offer Remote Assistance setting in the Details pane and click Properties. The Offer Remote Assistance Properties dialog box is displayed.

8. Select the Enabled option and then click the Show button. The Show Contents dialog box is displayed.

9. Click the Add button. The Add Item dialog box is displayed.

10. In the Enter The Item To Be Added text box, key **CONTOSO\Administrators** and then click OK.

11. Click OK in the Show Contents dialog box and click OK in the Offer Remote Assistance Properties dialog box.

12. Keep the Group Policy Object Editor console open.

Exercise 12.2	Configure Remote Desktop Through Group Policy
Overview	You will use Group Policy to allow all users to log on to their workstations remotely to work more efficiently from home. You decide to use Group Policy to turn on this setting for all users. You want all users to be able to redirect audio output to their remote machine.
Completion time	5 minutes

1. Continuing from the previous exercise, with the Group Policy Object Editor console open to edit the Remote GPO, expand Computer Configuration>Administrative Templates>Windows Components>Terminal Services>Terminal Server and select the Connections node.

2. In the Details pane, right-click Allow Users To Connect Remotely Using Terminal Services and click Properties. The Allow Users To Connect Remotely Using Terminal Services Properties dialog box is displayed.

3. Select the Enabled option and click OK.

4. Select the Device And Resource Redirection node in the console tree.

5. In the Details pane, right-click Allow Audio Redirection and click Properties. The Allow Audio Redirection Properties dialog box is displayed.

6. Select the Enabled option and click OK.

7. Close the Group Policy Object Editor console and the Group Policy Management console.

Exercise 12.3	Determine Effective File and Folder Permissions
Overview	You will check effective permissions for a folder. A user is having difficulty with her redirected desktop folders. As a first step in troubleshooting the issue, you check her (or her user group's) effective permissions for the redirected desktop folder on the server.
Completion time	5 minutes

1. Still logged on to your Windows Vista client as chrisa, click Start>All Programs>Accessories>Windows Explorer.

2. In Windows Explorer, if the menu bar is not visible, click Organize, Layout, Menu Bar.

3. From the Tools menu, select Map Network Drive. The Map Network Drive dialog box is displayed.

4. In the Folder text box, key **WinSrv03\Redirect** and click Finish.

5. In the folder tree, expand Computer>redirect (\\winsrv03). Right-click the Desktops folder and click Properties. The Desktops Properties dialog box is displayed.

6. Select the Security tab. Click the Advanced button. The Advanced Security Settings For Desktops dialog box is displayed.

7. Click the Effective Permissions tab, as shown in Figure 12-1.

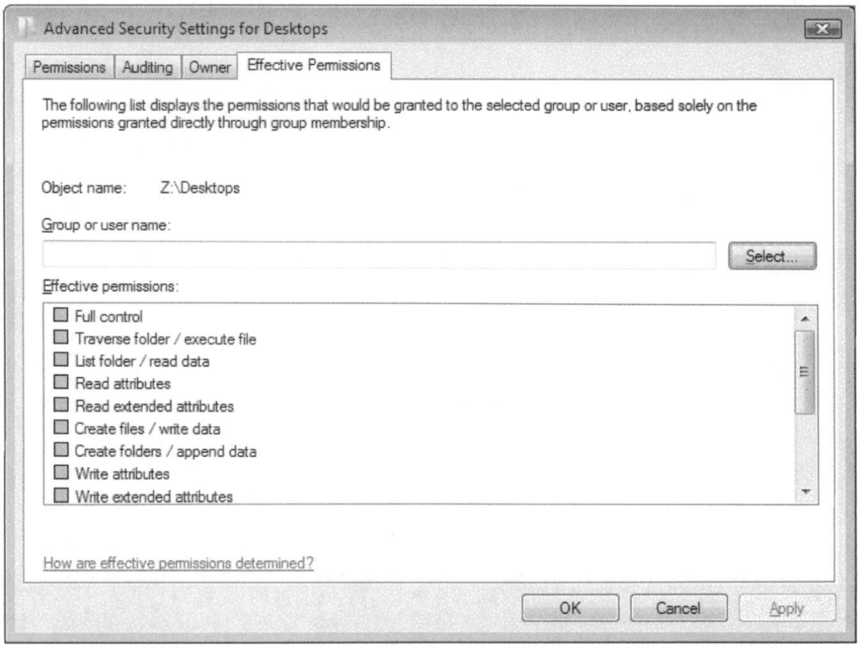

Figure 12-1
The Effective Permissions tab of the Advanced Security Settings for Desktops dialog box

8. Click Select. The Select User, Computer, Or Group dialog box is displayed. In the Enter The Object Name To Select text box, key **sheelaw** and then click Check Names.

9. Click OK. The effective permissions list is updated, displaying Sheela Word's permissions for the Redirect\Desktop folder on the server, as shown in Figure 12-2.

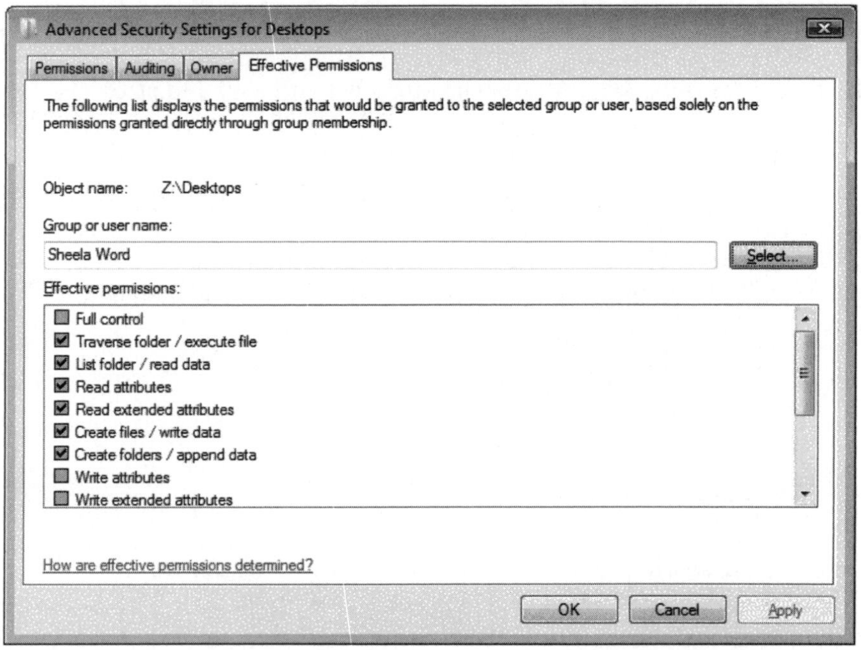

Figure 12-2
The Effective Permissions tab with Sheela Word's permissions listed

10. Close all open dialog boxes and windows.

Question 1	How can you check the effective permissions for an entire user group?

Exercise 12.4	Enable a User to Connect to a VPN Server
Overview	You will allow a user to connect to your server via dial-up or Virtual Private Network (VPN) connection. You want to allow Sheela Word to connect via VPN. You must enable this option on her user account.
Completion time	5 minutes

1. Log on to Windows Server 2003 with your administrator account (netadmin and p@ssw0rd).

2. Click Start, point to Administrative Tools, and then click Active Directory Users And Computers. The Active Directory Users And Computers console is displayed.

3. In the console tree, expand the contoso.com node and then click Users.

4. Double-click Sheela Word in the Details pane. The Sheela Word Properties dialog box is displayed.

5. Click the Dial-in tab. In the Remote Access Permission (Dial-in or VPN) section, select Allow Access, as shown in Figure 12-3. Click OK.

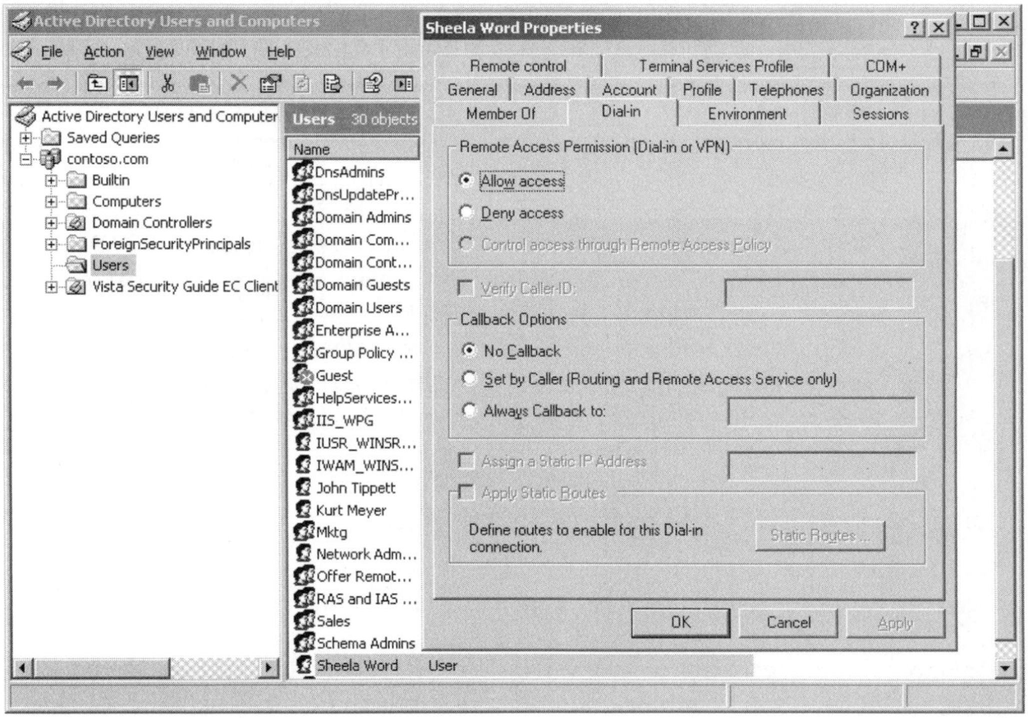

Figure 12-3
Allowing Remote Access Permission through the Active Directory Users And Computers console

6. Close the Active Directory Users And Computers console.

7. Stay logged on to the server and proceed to Exercise 12.5.

Exercise 12.5 Enable a Group to Connect to a VPN Server

Overview	You will allow a group of users to connect to your server via Virtual Private Network (VPN) connection. Because you want all employees in the Mktg group to connect directly to the enterprise network from home machines, use the Routing And Remote Access console to create a policy allowing members of the Mktg user group to connect to the VPN.
Completion time	10 minutes

> *To use the Routing And Remote Access console to configure a VPN server, the VPN server should have two networking interfaces installed. If your lab environment uses Virtual PC to host the server, you can configure two networking interfaces using a single physical network card. Otherwise, your server will need two physical network cards or a custom configuration to configure it as a VPN server.*

1. Continuing from the previous exercise and still logged on to Windows Server 2003, click Start, point to Administrative Tools, and then click Routing And Remote Access. The Routing And Remote Access console is displayed.

2. In the console tree, expand the WINSRV03 (local) node, right-click Remote Access Policies, and then click New Remote Access Policy. The New Remote Access Policy Wizard is displayed with the *Welcome To The New Remote Policy Wizard* page open.

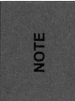

> *If you are unable to expand WINSRV03 in the Routing And Remote Access console, your server is not configured as a VPN Server. To configure WinSrv03 as a VPN server, go to http://articles.techrepublic.com and search for "Configure a Windows Server 2003 VPN on the server side" for details.*

3. Click Next. The *Policy Configuration Method* page is displayed.

4. Verify that the Use The Wizard To Set Up A Typical Policy For A Common Scenario option is selected. In the Policy Name text box, key **Marketing VPN Connections**. Click Next. The *Access Method* page is displayed.

5. Select the VPN option and click Next. The *User Or Group Access* page is displayed.

6. Select Group and then click the Add button. The Select Groups dialog box is displayed.

7. Key **mktg** in the Enter The Object Names To Select text box. Click Check Names, as shown in Figure 12-4, and then click OK.

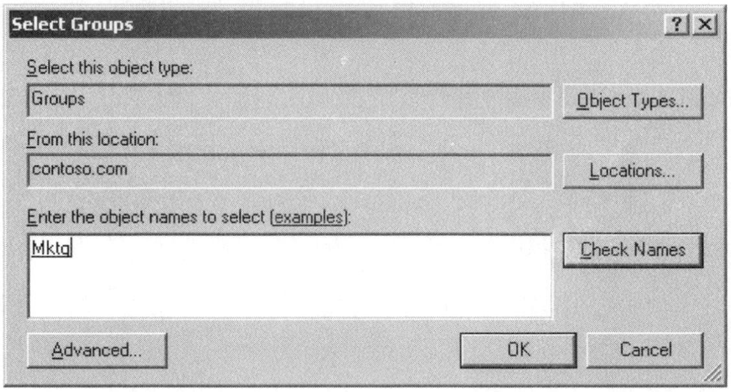

Figure 12-4
The Select Groups dialog box after clicking the Check Names button

8. Click Next. The *Authentication Methods* page is displayed.

9. Select Microsoft Encrypted Authentication Version 2 (MS-CHAPv2). Click Next. The *Policy Encryption Level* page is displayed.

10. Keep all the checkboxes selected and click Next. The *Completing the New Remote Access Policy Wizard* page is displayed.

11. Review the policy summary and then click Finish.

Exercise 12.6	Configure a VPN Client Connection
Overview	You will configure the connection for the user's home machine. For your users to connect from home to a VPN, their home machines must be configured with a VPN connection. You must teach users how to connect and disconnect from the network using the newly configured connection.
Completion time	10 minutes

Create a VPN Connection

1. Still logged on to your Windows Vista client as chrisa, click Start and then click Connect To. The Connect To A Network Wizard is displayed.

Because chrisa is not a member of the Mktg group, the Marketing VPN Connections policy you created earlier does not apply to chrisa's account. However, as an administrator, chrisa can use this exercise to walk users through the process when they are logged into their home computers.

2. Click the Set Up A Connection Or Network link. The *Choose A Connection Option* page is displayed.

3. Select Connect To A Workplace and then click Next. The *How Do You Want To Connect* page is displayed.

4. On the *How Do You Want To Connect* page, click Use My Internet Connection (VPN). The *Type The Internet Address To Connect To* page is displayed.

5. In the Internet Address text box, key **192.168.1.200** (or the appropriate IP address for WinSrv03 in your environment). In the Destination Name text box, key **Home to Office VPN Connection**. Select the Don't Connect Now; Just Set It Up So I Can Connect Later checkbox, as shown in Figure 12-5.

```
Connect to a workplace

Type the Internet address to connect to

Your network administrator can give you this address.

Internet address:       192.168.1.200

Destination name:       Home to Office VPN Connection


    ☐ Use a smart card

    ☐ Allow other people to use this connection
       This option allows anyone with access to this computer to use this connection.

    ☑ Don't connect now; just set it up so I can connect later


                                              [ Next ]   [ Cancel ]
```

Figure 12-5
The *Type The Internet Address To Connect To* page of the Connect To A Network Wizard

6. Click Next. The *Type Your User Name And Password* page is displayed.

7.   Key **sheelaw** in the User Name text box and key **p@ssw0rd** in the Password text box. Leave the Domain (Optional) text box blank. (The user can overwrite the entries you make in this window when they use the new connection.) Click Create. After the connection is created, the The *Connection Is Ready To Use* page is displayed. Click Close.

Use the New VPN Connection

8.   Click Start and then click Connect To. The Connect To A Network dialog box is displayed, as shown in Figure 12-6.

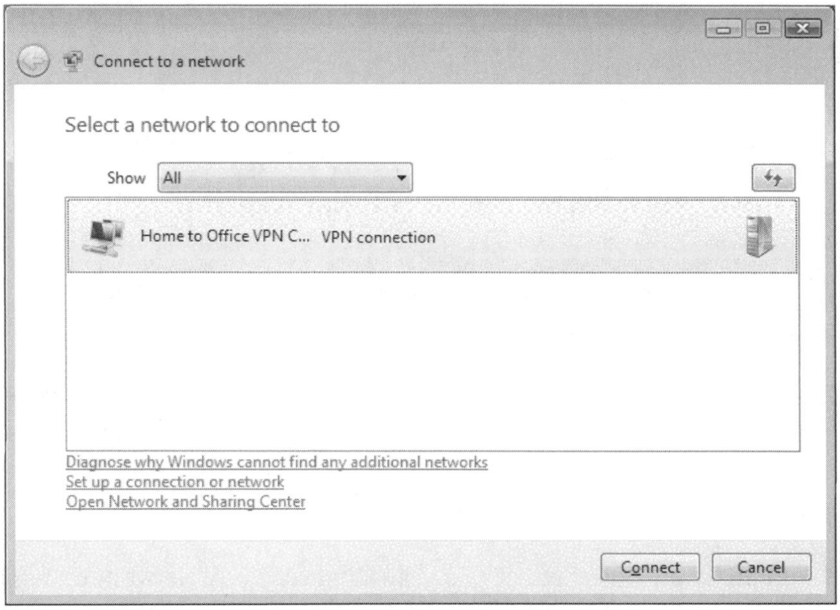

Figure 12-6
The Connect To A Network dialog box

9.   Select the connection and click Connect. The Connect Home To Office VPN Connection dialog box prompts you for a user name and password.

10.   The User Name text box should already contain sheelaw. Key **p@ssw0rd** in the Password text box and leave the Domain text box blank, as shown in Figure 12-7. Click Connect.

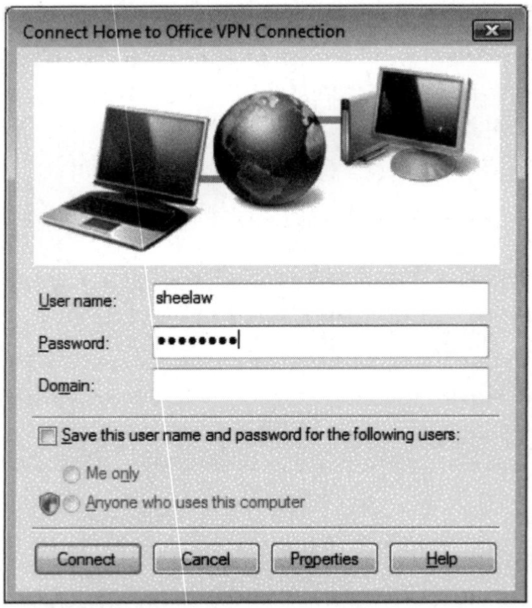

Figure 12-7
Entering the user name and password when connecting to a VPN connection

11. When the Successfully *Connected To Home To Office VPN Connection* page is displayed, click Close.

Disconnect a VPN Connection

12. Click Start and then click Connect To. The Connect To A Network dialog box is displayed. Select the connection through which you are currently connected and click Disconnect.

13. When the *Successfully Disconnected From Home To Office VPN Connection* page is displayed, click Close.

Question 2	*When you create a VPN client connection, which user name and password should you supply to the Connect To A Network Wizard? What if a different user wants to use the connection?*

Exercise 12.7	Start Windows Network Diagnostics
Overview	You will run the Windows Network Diagnostics (WND) utility. When you are troubleshooting a problematic network connection, the Windows Network Diagnostics utility can uncover problems and recommend solutions.
Completion time	5 minutes

1. Still logged on to your Windows Vista client as chrisa, click Start and then click Control Panel. Control Panel is displayed.

2. Under Network And Internet, click View Network Status And Tasks.

3. In the tasks list, click Diagnose And Repair. A WND message box is displayed and indicates progress. WND will report that it could not find a problem (see Figure 12-8), or it will tell you that it did find a problem and offer options for troubleshooting or resolving the problem.

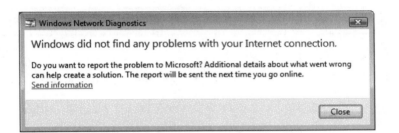

Figure 12-8
A working network connection

LAB REVIEW QUESTIONS

Completion time	10 minutes

1. If you want a user to be able to work from home, what are two possible options for the user to connect to the enterprise network remotely?

2. For a user to connect remotely using VPN, what two items must be configured? Which two tools do you use to configure these options?

3. List two tools you can use to troubleshoot networking problems and describe how you run the tools.

LAB CHALLENGE: TROUBLESHOOT NETWORKING WITH COMMAND-LINE TOOLS

Completion time	20 minutes

Experiment with running the following command-line tools to familiarize yourself with how they work and with the expected output:

- Ping
- IPConfig
- Net view
- Tracert
- PathPing
- NSlookup

After experimenting with each command, redirect each tool's output into a file. (Supply appropriate arguments for Ping, Traceert, and PathPing.) For example, key the **Ipconfig > results_ipconfig.txt** command, which will save the output in the results_ipconfig.txt file.

Copy all of your results files to the \\winsrv03\Redirect\Pictures folder. (Your instructor might specify an alternate location, possibly with subfolders for each student.)

LAB 13
SUPPORTING AND MAINTAINING DESKTOP APPLICATIONS

This lab contains the following exercises and activities:

SCENARIO

You have decided to use Group Policy to distribute software to the users at Contoso. The first application you plan to roll out enables employees in the sales department to collaborate on a project. First you must create a Distributed File System network share that contains the application to be distributed. Then you will set Group Policy to distribute the application to members of the Sales users group. Users will install the software by using Control Panel. You test this for a particular user. Later, when you need to upgrade the application, you distribute the upgrade by using the same system.

After completing this lab, you will be able to:

- Create a network folder.

- Create a network share by using the Distributed File System service.

- Apply Group Policy to selected user groups by using a filter.

- Distribute applications to users via Group Policy.

- Test the distribution of an application.

- Distribute upgrades for an already distributed application.

Estimated lab time: 55 minutes

Exercise 13.1	Create a DFS Root to Distribute Software via Group Policy
Overview	You will create a network share and then use it as a Distributed Software (DFS) root so that you can move the actual bits among servers as needed. You will add an application installation package to the network share for distribution.
Completion time	10 minutes

Create a Network Folder

1. Log on to Windows Server 2003 with your administrator account by keying **netadmin** in the User Name text box and keying **p@ssw0rd** in the Password text box.

2. Click Start>Windows Explorer. Windows Explorer opens. Expand My Computer>C:\ in the Folders pane and then select the Clients folder. Right-click

an empty area in the Details pane, point to New in the context menu, and select Folder. Change the name of the new folder by immediately keying **Software** and pressing Enter.

3. Right-click the new Software folder and select Properties. The Software Properties dialog box is displayed.

4. Select the Security tab and then click Add. The Select Users, Computers Or Groups dialog box is displayed.

5. Key **authenticated users** in the Enter Object Names To Select list box, click Check Names, and then click OK.

6. On the Security tab of the Software Properties dialog box, select Authenticated Users in the Group Or User Names list and then verify that the Read & Execute, List Folder Contents, and Read permissions are selected, as shown in Figure 13-1.

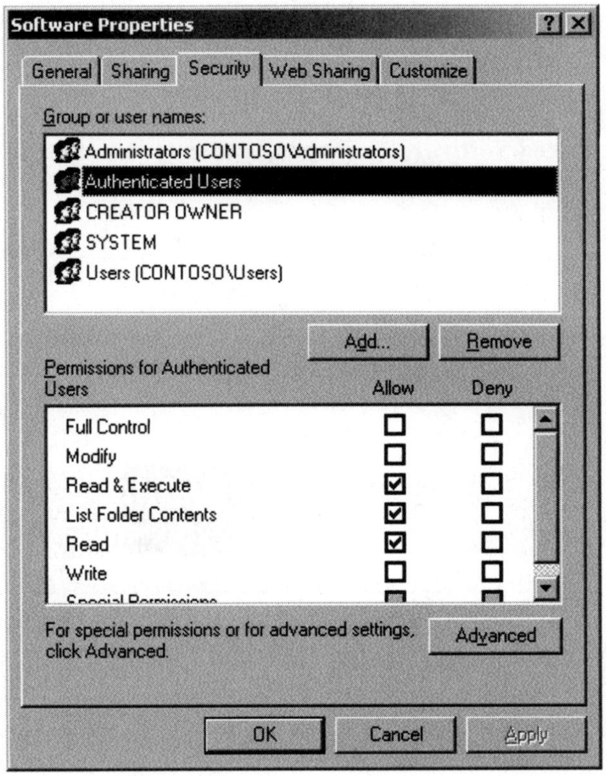

Figure 13-1
Security permissions for the new Software folder

7. Click OK to close the Software Properties dialog box.

Create the DFS Root

8. On Windows Server 2003, select Start>Administrative Tools>Distributed File System. The Distributed File System console is displayed.

9. Right-click the Distributed File System node in the Distributed File System console and then select New Root. The New Root Wizard is displayed.

10. Click Next. The *Root Type* page of the New Root Wizard is displayed.

11. Verify that the Domain Root option is selected and click Next. The *Host Domain* page of the New Root Wizard is displayed.

12. The Domain Name and Trusting Domains text boxes should already list contoso.com. Click Next. The *Host Server* page of the New Root Wizard is displayed.

13. Key **WinSrv03** in the Server Name text box and click Next. The *Root Name* page of the New Root Wizard is displayed.

14. In the Root Name text box, key **Software**. In the Comments text box, key **DFS Root for Distributed Software Packages**, as shown in Figure 13-2.

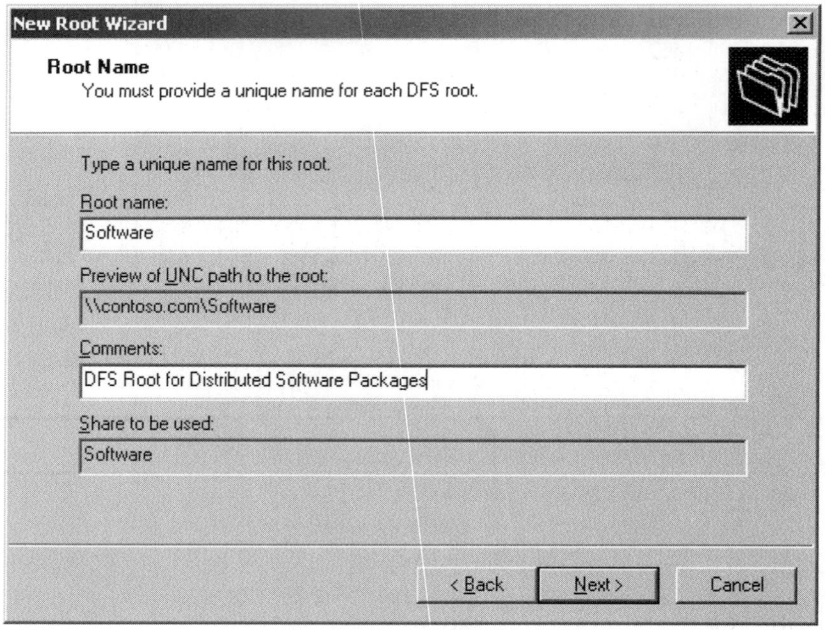

Figure 13-2
Creating the DFS Root for the shared Software folder

15. Click Next. The *Root Share* page of the New Root Wizard is displayed.

16. Click Browse. The Browse For Folder dialog box is displayed.

17. Expand the C:\Clients folders, select the Software folder, and click OK.

18. On the *Root Share* page, click Next.

19. On the *Completing Root Wizard* page, click Finish.

20. Close the Distributed File System console.

Add a Software Package to the Network Share

21. Download (using Internet Explorer) or copy (using Windows Explorer) the SharedView.msi file to the Software folder you have just created.

> *Your instructor might provide you with an alternate msi file to download or copy. The SharedView.msi file mentioned in the text book was created for a beta version of Microsoft SharedView. The file is available at www.connect.microsoft.com.*

22. Close all open windows and log off of the server as netadmin.

Question 1	*What is the advantage of using DFS when creating a shared network folder?*

Exercise 13.2	**Create Software Categories**
Overview	You will mark an application to be distributed as belonging to a particular category. This allows you to group distributed software so that you do not need to create separate distribution rules for each new application you want to distribute.
Completion time	10 minutes

1. Log on to your Windows Vista client as chrisa. (Key **contoso\chrisa** in the first box, key **p@ssw0rd** in the second box, and then press Enter.)

2. Create a new GPO as instructed in Exercise 3.2, giving the new GPO the name Shared View Distribution GPO. Verify that the new GPO is linked and enabled as instructed in Exercise 3.2.

3. In the Group Policy Management console (GPMC), right-click the Shared View Distribution GPO link under the contoso.com node and then select Edit. The Group Policy Object Editor console is displayed.

4. In the Group Policy Object Editor, in the console tree, expand User Configuration>Software Settings.

5. Right-click Software Installation in the console tree and select Properties. The Software Installation Properties dialog box is displayed.

6. Select the Categories tab and then click Add. The Enter New Category dialog box is displayed.

7. Key **Collaboration** and click OK.

8. Click Add again to redisplay the Enter New Category dialog box. Key **Marketing** and click OK.

9. In the Software Installation Properties dialog box, click the Advanced tab and then select Uninstall The Applications When They Fall Out Of The Scope Of Management check box. Click OK.

10. Close the Group Policy Object Editor console, but keep the Group Policy Management console open and proceed to Exercise 13.3.

Exercise 13.3	Filter Group Policy by Security Group
Overview	You will set the Software Distribution GPO to apply only to the Sales user group. Each user group can be assigned its own set of applications to install.
Completion time	5 minutes

1. Continuing from the previous exercise, in the Group Policy Management console, select the Shared View Distribution GPO in the console tree under the contoso.com node. A Group Policy Management Console message box might be displayed, warning you that changes you make will affect all locations to which this GPO is linked. Click OK to dismiss the message box.

2. In the Details pane of the Group Policy Management console, on the Scope tab, you will see Security Filtering in the bottom half of the window. Click Add under the Security Filtering section. The Select User, Computer, Or Group dialog box is displayed.

3. In the Enter The Object Name list box, key **Sales**. Click Check Names and then click OK.

4.   Select Authenticated Users in the Name list under the Security Filtering section and click Remove. A Group Policy Management message box prompts you to confirm the removal.

5.   Click OK to remove this delegation privilege. You should see only the Sales group under the Security Filtering section.

Question 2	How does categorizing a distributed application make your job easier?

Exercise 13.4	Publish Application Packages to Users via Group Policy
Overview	You will set up an application to be available for installation by users in the Sales user group. The actual bits for the application will reside on a shared network folder. Users will be able to use Control Panel to select available software to install on their client.
Completion time	10 minutes

1.   Still logged on to your Windows Vista client as chrisa, in the Group Policy Management console, right-click the Shared View Distribution GPO link under the contoso.com node and then select Edit. The Group Policy Object Editor console is displayed.

2.   In the Group Policy Object Editor, in the console tree, expand User Configuration>Software Settings, right-click Software installation, select New, and then select Package. The Open dialog box is displayed.

3.   In the File Name box, key **contoso.com\software** and then click Open. The SharedView MSI package is listed in the Open dialog box, as shown in Figure 13-3.

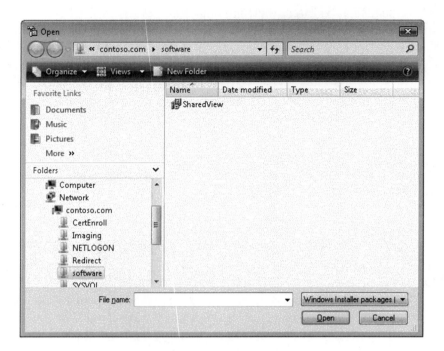

Figure 13-3
The Open dialog box with the SharedView MSI package listed

4. Select SharedView in the file list and then click Open again. The Deploy Software dialog box is displayed.

5. Verify that the Published option is selected and click OK.

6. Select the Software Installation node in the console tree, right-click the Microsoft SharedView (Beta) package in the Details pane, and then select Properties.

NOTE

After publishing the package, it might take a few minutes before the Microsoft SharedView (Beta) package appears in the Details pane. If you don't see the package, try closing and opening the Group Policy Object Editor console. If necessary, open the file Properties for the SharedView.msi file on the server and click the Unblock button near the bottom of the General tab.

7. Select the Categories tab. Under Available Categories, select Collaboration and click Select. Collaboration will be displayed under Selected Categories, as shown in Figure 13-4. Click OK.

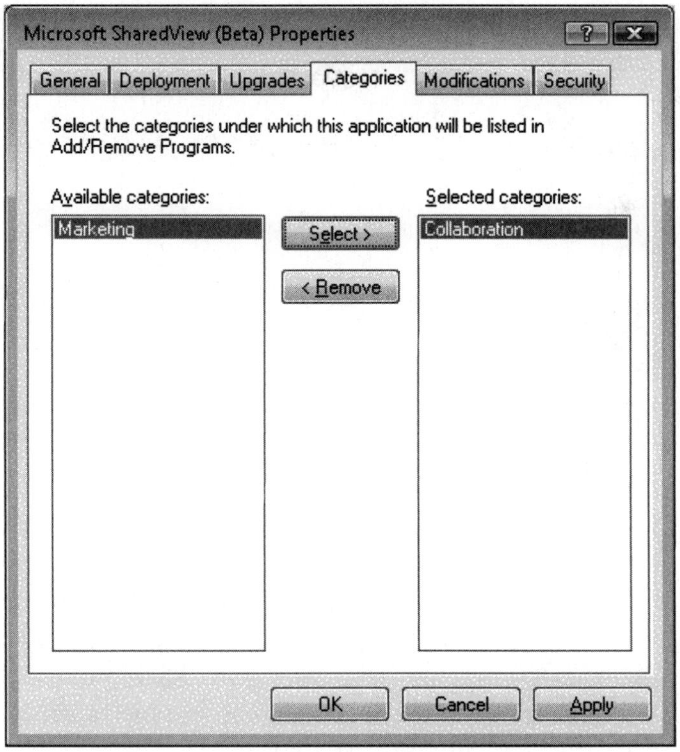

Figure 13-4
The Categories tab of the Microsoft SharedView (Beta) Properties dialog box

8. Close the Group Policy Object Editor console and the Group Policy Management console.

Exercise 13.5	Test a Published Application
Overview	You will log on as a user in the Sales user group and use Control Panel to install available distributed application packages.
Completion time	10 minutes

1. Still logged on to your Windows Vista client as chrisa, click Start and then click the right arrow to the right of the Search box. Click Switch User. A startup window is displayed.

2. Press Ctrl + Alt + Delete. To log on as John Tippett, key **johnt** in the User Name text box, key **p@ssw0rd** in the Password text box, and then press Enter.

3. From the Start menu, open the Control Panel and select Programs. The Programs section of Control Panel is displayed.

4. Under Get Programs, select Install A Program From The Network. A list of installable programs is displayed in the Name section, as shown in Figure 13-5.

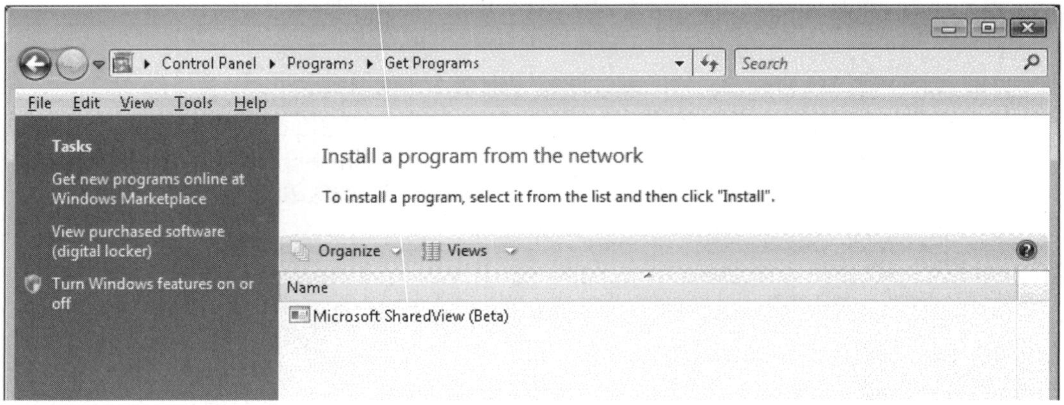

Figure 13-5
The Microsoft SharedView (Beta) installation package is listed in the Get Programs section of Control Panel for John Tippett

5. Select Microsoft SharedView (Beta) in the Name section and then click Install. The Windows Installer begins the Microsoft SharedView (Beta) Setup installation. Click Cancel to cancel the installation and then click Yes to confirm your decision.

6. Log off as John Tippett.

Question 3	When you use Group Policy to distribute applications, does the user always have to use Control Panel to install the application? If not, when and how is the application installed?

Exercise 13.6	Upgrade an Application via Group Policy
Overview	You will configure a distributed application package as an upgrade to an already distributed application.
Completion time	10 minutes

1. Continuing from the previous exercise, you are presented with a startup window.

2. Press Ctrl + Alt + Delete. To reconnect to Chris Ashton's log-on session, key **chrisa** in the User Name textbox, key **p@ssw0rd** in the Password text box, and then press Enter.

3. In the Start Search text box, key **gpmc.msc** and then press Ctrl + Shift + Enter to start the Group Policy Management console (GPMC) using administrator credentials. A User Account Control dialog box is displayed.

4. Key your administrator name and password (**netadmin** and **p@ssw0rd**). Click OK. The Group Policy Management console is displayed.

5. Expand Forest: contoso.com>Domains>contoso.com. Right-click the Shared View Distribution GPO policy and click Edit. Expand User Configuration>Software Settings and then right-click the Software Installation node, select New, and select Package. The Open dialog box is displayed.

 For this exercise, assume that the SharedView.msi file contains an upgrade to the SharedView software package that was set up for distribution in earlier exercises.

6. Select the SharedView MSI package and click Open. The Deploy Software dialog box is displayed.

7. Select the Advanced option and click OK. Select the Upgrades tab, select the Required Upgrade For Existing Packages checkbox (as shown in Figure 13-6), and click OK.

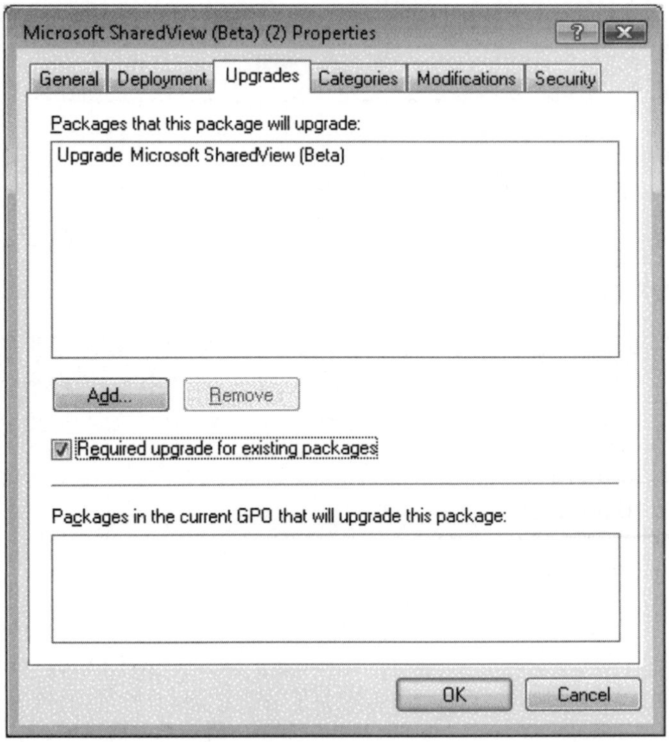

Figure 13-6
Specifying a required upgrade on the Upgrades tab of the package Properties dialog box

8. Close the Group Policy Object Editor console and the Group Policy Management console.

LAB REVIEW QUESTIONS

Completion time	10 minutes

1. In broad terms, what are the two primary steps necessary to set up Group Policy to distribute an application? What "frills" were added to these steps in this lab?

2. In this lab, even though the SharedView application package was contained in a network share named \\WinSrv03\Software, what DFS name can clients use to refer to the network share?

3. In general, when you distribute an upgrade to an application, will all application users be required to upgrade their applications?

LAB CHALLENGE: DETERMINE THE PRODUCT CODE GUID FOR A PUBLISHED PACKAGE

Completion time	5 minutes

Following the "Identifying Packages by Product Code" procedure Lesson 13 in the text book, use the Advanced Diagnostic Information section of the deployment package Properties dialog box to find the Product Code GUID for the package you created in this lab. Record your package's GUID and submit it to your instructor.

NOTES

NOTES

NOTES

NOTES

NOTES

NOTES

NOTES

NOTES

NOTES

NOTES